RESTORING TRUST IN GOVERNANCE

INDIA'S 2020'S CHALLENGE

M G WARRIER

INDIA • SINGAPORE • MALAYSIA

Notion Press

No.8, 3rd Cross Street,
CIT Colony, Mylapore,
Chennai, Tamil Nadu – 600004

First Published by Notion Press 2020
Copyright © M G Warrier 2020
All Rights Reserved.

ISBN 978-1-63633-589-6

This book has been published with all efforts taken to make the material error-free after the consent of the author. However, the author and the publisher do not assume and hereby disclaim any liability to any party for any loss, damage, or disruption caused by errors or omissions, whether such errors or omissions result from negligence, accident, or any other cause.

While every effort has been made to avoid any mistake or omission, this publication is being sold on the condition and understanding that neither the author nor the publishers or printers would be liable in any manner to any person by reason of any mistake or omission in this publication or for any action taken or omitted to be taken or advice rendered or accepted on the basis of this work. For any defect in printing or binding the publishers will be liable only to replace the defective copy by another copy of this work then available.

To
My Support Team
comprising
Sudha
Kiran
Smitha
Reshmy
Govind
and
Vihaan

Contents

Preface   7

Section I – Development Issues

Agenda for Modi 2.0 (2019–24)	11
NYAY: Can it Bring Justice (*Nyay*) to the Poor?	19
Privatizing Public Sector	26
India's Gold Gets a Makeover	29

Section II – Banking for Economic Recovery & Growth

RBI's Role as Confidence Booster	39
Restoring Trust: India's 2020's Challenge	47
Focus Shifts to Growth at RBI	56
Multiple Objectives, One Policy	69
RBI's Functional Freedom	85
Reserve Bank of India: What Lies Ahead?	92
India's Central Bank: Challenges Galore I	98
India's Central Bank: Challenges Galore II	106
Reserve Bank's Policy Perceptions I	115

Reserve Bank's Policy Perceptions II	124
Rating RBI's Policy: Beyond Rate Cuts	130
RBI's Monetary Policy: In the Right Direction	143
Monetary Policy II: RBI Takes Charge	149

Section III –
Professionalizing Financial System

PSBs in Recovery Room: Multiple Prescriptions	161
What Do PSBs Want?	170
Prompt Corrective Action: Need of the Hour	179
Public Sector Banks: Readying to Meet New Challenges	192
FDI in Indian Banks	197
Changing Phases of Debt Restructuring	201
Handling Bank Frauds	206
Strengthen Reserve Bank of India	213

Preface

This is my third book with focus on banking and finance. As economic reforms in India are moving fast especially with emphasis on cleansing and consolidating financial sector, I felt some urgency in publishing this book as a companion volume to my 2018 book "India's Decade of Reforms." This book was scheduled to be published during the first half of 2020. The situation that emerged with the COVID19 Pandemic delayed the publication by almost four months. The impact of the recent developments on Indian Economy, to the extent perceivable now, has been covered at the appropriate places in this book. Needless to say, as of now, it is the fire-fighting stage and it will take longer to quantify losses and put in place what one may call a comprehensive "Post-Pandemic Rehabilitation Plan." Present debates are all speculative in nature.

My first book "Banking, Reforms and Corruption: Development Issues in the 21st Century India" published in 2014 (Sampark, Kolkatta) has been republished in 2018 as eBook with a change in title to "Chasing Inclusive Growth: Reforms for Financial Inclusion" indicative of the book's subject focus. The Notion Press, Chennai published my second book "India's Decade of Reforms: Reserve Bank of India at Central Stage" in print and eBook versions of both my books during 2018.

Amazon Kindle Direct Publishing has brought out some of my non-banking/non-fiction books including Scrambled Monologues, Savings for Survival (a short book on Personal Finance), Ants and Honeybees: Life's Perceptions and Reflections and Assorted Letters of Dissent as eBooks, some of which are also available in print.

Some of the chapters finding a place in this book are based on my articles published in the monthly Business & Finance magazine, The Global ANALYST (Published by Iupindia, a division of the Institute of Chartered Financial Analysts of India – ICFAI, Hyderabad).

The book is organized in three sections.

Section I on Development Issues cover agenda for Modi 2.0 (2019–24), some aspects of universal basic minimum income and the relevance of NYAY, pros and cons of privatizing public sector and India's approach towards gold management.

Section II on 'Banking for Growth' covers RBI's role in confidence boosting, monetary policy since the setting up of Monetary Policy Committee (MPC), some aspects of policy challenges before the Reserve Bank of India, need for a strong central bank, relationship issues between RBI and GOI in the context of formulation and implementation of monetary and fiscal policies and general perceptions about the impact of changes in RBI's policy rates on financial market.

In Section III 'Professionalizing Financial System' we look at measures being taken to professionalize and strengthen the Financial Sector with focus on regulation and supervision of the banking system.

I thank my family, friends and the team at Notion Press who supported me in publishing this book.

M G Warrier

Mumbai

October 2, 2020

SECTION I – DEVELOPMENT ISSUES

Agenda for Modi 2.0 (2019–24)

NYAY: Can it bring justice (Nyay) to the poor?

Privatizing public sector

India's gold getting a makeover

Agenda for Modi 2.0 (2019–24)

Elections 2019, which gave a massive mandate for a second term for Prime Minister Narendra Modi, will remain a landmark in India's electoral and political history. Though the political leadership is yet to assimilate the lessons from the post-independence history of India, the average Indian voter is today more aware of his responsibilities and has perfected the art of deciding the best among the available options.

We are paying the price for not cultivating a participative democratic process right from the time of independence. The then Indian National Congress considered governance as a responsibility transferred to that party by the British. This misunderstanding led to suppression of opposition till early 1960's. Had we consciously allowed a healthy opposition to grow in an orderly manner, the present misconception that the role of opposition is to oppose the government of the day might not have grown to the present proportions.

People of India too, till the "India Against Corruption" days, considered governing the country as the prerogative of some celebrity leaders, though the architects of the Indian Constitution had clarity of purpose and gave the Constitution to "We, The People"

The 21st Century awakening around India Against Corruption movement which kindled hopes in the GenNext too fizzled out with the Aam Admi Party (AAP) making a hurry to grab power. Unless a people's movement infuses some discipline in the political leadership, it is doubtful whether the debates in the media or efforts from a few concerned citizens will be able to pull the country out of the political mess in which it has landed itself.

The earlier the political leadership consciously minimized the dependence on emotional vote banks and allowed literacy level to go up and ensured that votes are cast based on informed debates about national level priorities, the better for the country. To make this happen, people's trust in rule of law and constitutional institutions need to be restored first. We need to revisit these issues periodically.

For now, let us repose trust in the members of the Lok Sabha and the Rajya Sabha who have the mandate to oversee governance and make changes in legislations for upholding Indian Constitution and ensuring economic development. With reinforced confidence the Modi 2.0 government in Delhi is taking forward the NDA agenda announced in the 2014 Independence Day speech given by Narendra Modi. Then, the Prime Minister symbolically referred to the Planning Commission as a house in disrepair needing reconstruction. Today, many more institutions including those in judiciary, financial sector and statutory bodies responsible for carrying out different crucial roles and responsibilities are awaiting thorough overhaul.

The resolve to do this much, and more in the coming years was evident in Prime Minister Narendra Modi's maiden speech after the decisive electoral victory on May 23, 2019. He said:

- His government will not do any work with bad intent or motive
- There will be only two castes, those who are poor and those who work for the uplift of the poor
- The country should be run through consensus and democratic spirit
- This election victory was a win for the aspirations of the people, farmers and the middle class.

Some areas which need immediate attention and 'out of the box' approaches, that come to mind, are discussed here.

I Resources Management

Though our country has only one-third the geographical area as compared to US with more than 3 times that country's population, we are blessed with much more resources and a much better weather cycle. Also, we are yet to appropriately exploit the potential of our skilled workforce.

(a) Land and Buildings

We should immediately take up a survey of usable land and buildings in cities and towns with a population of 5 lakhs and above. The survey should cover Rashtrapathi Bhavan to temple/mosque/church premises with an objective of optimal use for public advantage. For example, the possibility of ministerial bungalows spread over the whole city getting substituted by residential complexes in the vicinity of Parliament House, Secretariats or Legislative Houses can be considered. The excess land and buildings that will get released will be worth billions which can be redeployed for economic development. The city traffic also will become smooth.

(b) Domestic Gold Stocks

Gold Management needs a makeover. Domestic gold stock with individuals and institutions (including religious bodies) need to be accounted and mainstreamed for nation's benefit.

Through an amendment to its earlier instructions the Reserve Bank of India has expanded the ambit of gold-monetization scheme during 2019 to enable charitable institutions and temples/religious bodies, among others, to invest their gold stock under the Scheme. The revised instructions give a new avenue for productive deployment of idle domestic gold stock. This is a welcome move from RBI. The new entities which have become eligible to invest their gold stock under the scheme need to be educated about the advantages of mainstreaming their gold stock. Issues of trust, faith, emotion and sheer laziness to take responsibility on the part of voluntary social workers who generally manage the affairs of Trusts and Boards of Management of religious bodies need to be addressed with care and deftness.

Past experience shows that the organizations do not spontaneously volunteer to redeploy their assets including gold and jewelry, even if the investment fetches substantial returns. Perhaps, Tirupathi and Siddhivinayak (Mumbai) are the only temples which have already availed of the facility to deposit substantial portions of their gold in banks and are earning income from such deposits. Some of the other temples/religious bodies are sometimes secretive about even the quantity of gold in their vaults. Governments' eye on every asset as an income source (read tax) also is behind such fear complex.

According to media reports, in recent years, Tirupathi temple had gold deposits of over 4000 kg with two banks fetching the equivalent of the value of around 80 kg gold as interest per annum.

If Centre is serious about mainstreaming domestic stock of investible gold, massive efforts will have to be made to create awareness among the people about the benefits that will accrue to the country's economy by deploying part of the surface gold stock productively. The availability of sovereign guarantee for the gold invested, professional handling of conversion of gold and timely payment of interest and return of gold or value of gold will have to be ensured by central/state governments. The existence of such protection and facilities should also be publicized in a business-like manner to attract investment.

Perhaps India may be alone in the world to sustain the dubious distinction of grossly mismanaging domestic gold stock the country has been holding for centuries in huge quantities, in multiple forms, and in various places and simultaneously struggling to control smuggling of gold, evading taxes etc.. When the population starved and died as a consequence of bad governance or as victims of nature's wrath, Indian rulers allowed use of huge quantities of gold (a) to be wasted for gold-plating of roofs, flag-masts, and statues and (b) to be held in underground vaults, hidden and unaccounted, as unproductive 'assets.' A positive change in approach to gold is perceivable from the second half of the last decade.

Errol D'Souza, Director, IIM, Ahmedabad in his note recorded in the 3rd Annual Report (2017–18) of the India Gold Policy Centre had this to say about gold management in India:

"As a macroeconomist, I uphold the view that integrating gold with India's broader economic vision is the touchstone for India's gold policy and gold markets. The foremost is adopting 'Make in India' policy which should address unexplored gold stocks below the ground, optimal use of gold stocks in circulation, and mobilize gold holdings held by individuals in lockers and temples."

At this late hour, GOI need to understand the significance of the treasure in the form of gold stock with institutions and individuals lying idle in the country. As a short-term plan, concrete measures should be initiated for putting a substantial portion of the domestic gold stock to productive use in the next 5 years. This will reduce the country's gold import bill considerably. This can be achieved by:

a. Making a realistic assessment of gold stock remaining idle in the country

b. Providing incentives to holders of gold stock to properly account for the stock with them

c. Making gold deposits with banks remunerative

d. Introducing gold-backed financial instruments which are not dependent on imported gold (The tiny instruments now available in the form of Gold ETFs, gold coins and Sovereign Gold Bonds are indirectly dependent on import and have not attracted significant investor-interest)

e. Quickly arrange for infrastructure, technology support and linkages for gold refining and certification facilities of international standard

Reserve Bank of India also need to convert the entire gold stock with the central bank to purer variety conforming to internationally acceptable standards. As gold becomes really a liquid asset, banks can be encouraged to maintain part of the Statutory Liquid Reserves (SLR) in gold. If this happens, a new chapter in the country's gold management will unfold. It is distressing to remember the 1991 'gold pledge' episode to save the country from a payment default when the forex reserves of the country had touched its nadir. Think of the agony of a central bank Governor being forced to 'ship' a small portion of gold in the central bank vault for pledging to draw a small amount of dollars. Even though the gold lying with Bank of England has long been freed of pledge, it was not considered necessary to physically ship the bullion back to India.

It should have been for valid reasons that options like selling a portion of gold stock or borrowing dollars against 'stock' of gold would have been dropped. Let us forget all that. But, let us remember, if the stock of gold in India was of internationally acceptable standard, things would have been different.

(c) Long Coastal Areas

India's long coastal areas remain underexploited. More Mini-ports, fishing harbours, tourism development, use of sea-belt for transportation of people and goods are all areas needing attention.

(d) Forests

Forest mapping, planned re-forestation, development of medicinal plant gardens in and around existing forests and commercial exploitation of forest produce without destroying environment need to be prioritized.

(e) Workforce

Workforce in India is in disarray for various historic reasons. Privatization of public services and outsourcing of work by organizations reducing the number of regular employees have affected job security in the short term and social security in the long term. Remuneration for every day's work should factor in the concept of fair wage comprising living wage and post-job survival costs.

II More Issues which Need Prioritization

There is something glaringly missing in management of resources and finance by Government of India and state governments, and that is planning. This is affecting smooth implementation of schemes and in some situations, effective functioning of institutions. Illustratively:

HR Issues in Financial Sector and Felt need for an Indian Financial Sector Service

Reserve Bank of India (RBI) can be a case study to understand how interlinked are HR issues with the functional efficiency of public sector organizations. Recently, RBI has merged some departments concerned with supervision and regulation of different categories of institutions in the financial sector and is presently in the process of inducting expertise by making direct recruitments at higher levels. The dilution of expertise in departments other than the Monetary Policy and Statistics Departments has a historic background.

Till early 1970's RBI had specialized departments for functions needing specialization. In 1972, combined seniority was introduced for some of the large departments and inter-mobility reduced the chances for development of expertise by remaining in the same work areas. Present effort is to induct experts from outside to compensate for this.

A better option would be to have an All India Financial Sector Service similar to Indian Civil Services or Tata Administrative Service with inter-mobility among finance ministries (Central and states), statutory bodies like **RBI, NABARD** and other statutory organizations, as also banks and financial institutions in public and private sectors.

Indian Pension System

With the introduction of NPS effective January 1, 2004, all is not well on the Indian pension front. Review for an overhaul is overdue. Cost of post-retiral life need to be factored-in, in the wage structure of regular employees in government, PSUs and in private sector.

Agricultural Income Tax

A consensus has to be reached to tax agricultural income above a reasonably high threshold level.

Kisan Samman

Doling out the paltry amount of Rs. 17 or Rs. 18 per day to farmers below the poverty line is an insult to the Indian farming community. What is needed is to plug the leakages in pricing of farm produce between the farm gate and the consumer. Once a reasonable farm gate price for the produce is assured, the present generation of workers know to extract their share as wages. This can be achieved by promoting cooperatives for production, processing and marketing.

Funding Government Expenditure

GOI, of late, has been dipping too deep into the pockets of PSUs and GOI-owned bodies like RBI to meet shortfalls in revenue. This approach will definitely get sympathy from taxpayers and corporates. Taxpayers' burden will be less to the extent GOI mobilizes resources from elsewhere and corporates can delay or deny repayments, if GOI make good the losses suffered by their creditors. But these are temporary reliefs and the country cannot delay mapping of domestic resources and ensuring distributive justice beyond a point.

Works in Progress on the Economic Front

We should listen first to experts' views on what they think are the immediate possible measures to put the Indian Economy on a high growth trajectory. A beginner's guide which gives illustrative notes on works in progress on the economic front is available in book form authored by experts who were and are associated with policy formulation/implementation in their work areas. I am referring to the book "What The Economy Needs Now" (April 2019) edited by Abhijit Banerjee, Gita Gopinath, Raghuram Rajan and Mihir Sharma. The book lists major issues facing Indian Economy needing immediate attention: Rising unemployment, Banking crisis, falling GDP, Farmers' unrest et al and goes on to discuss solutions to the vexing problems like labour reforms, healthcare, education and environment.

NYAY: Can it Bring Justice (*Nyay*) to the Poor?

One fine morning during the second week of March 2019, Indian Elite woke up and remembered an old Chinese proverb they had long forgotten about. The context:

The announcement of Nyunatam Aay Yojana (NYAY), a scheme proposed to be included in the Congress Manifesto for Election, 2019, by the Congress President Rahul Gandhi.

The proverb:

"Give a man a fish, and you feed him for a day. Teach a man to fish, and you feed him for a lifetime"

My friend Mohandas, a veteran central banker from Chennai had this to say about NYAY and the proverb:

"Now we may have to give him not only training to fish, but also a

Fishing Rod. For deep sea Fishing he may require a Motor boat costing about Rs. 10 to 20 lakhs! He has to be supported during the lean season for about 2 months when deep sea Fishing is banned to enable fishes to grow and for breeding purposes. We have to save the Indian farmer from committing Suicide. We have to save him from the clutches of the village money lenders. We have to support him during crop failure by giving free Crop Insurance. Indian agriculturist is born in debt, lives in debt, dies in debt and bequeaths debt. In India the poor becomes poorer and the rich becomes richer. We have to break this trend by giving the poor proper free education, better skill-development, jobs for all educated youth by promoting healthy industrial growth. The unskilled workforce should be fully utilized for jobs for which they are necessary and suitable, like building roads, desilting tanks and lakes as also several other manual work which can be performed by giving them some orientation. They too should be paid 'living wage' which will be much higher than the proposed dole which is called NYAY, and in many cases, the present statutory minimum wage! No able-bodied person should be allowed to beg, or receive doles, even if political expediency discovers conduits like NYAY"

It is not a question of whether the dole out is workable or not. It is a question of human dignity and prestige. Citizens would not like to take a government dole without doing any job. The very idea of encouraging idlers and beggars in the country is not welcome. It is insult to human dignity.

Having said that, a "Minimum Income Guarantee Scheme" is an idea worth pursuing and therefore, the debate on NYAY may survive election after election, irrespective of fortunes of political alliances.

As part of his media interactions for promoting his new book "The Third Pillar," former RBI governor Dr. Raghuram Rajan was also seen justifying NYAY (Hindi word for justice), leaving the audience wondering whether he is still on theory and doesn't want to go deep into the ground level realities of 'poverty cultivation' in India. One gets an impression that his own research for putting together "The Third Pillar" hovering around sophisticated economic theories and history, did not go deep into the present realities of urban and rural India.

In India, the elite political leadership which controls all the 'pillars' of governance, is still comfortable to retain a target 'catchment area' of people below poverty line poor and illiterate, to ensure availability of cheap labour (now rechristened as 'outsourced work') in different sectors. It is in this context that we are prepared to dole out a portion of taxpayers' money to keep a 'reserve' of illiterate and idle people who will be available on call at starvation wages to do unskilled work without any demand for fair wages.

The media and the analysts (economists included) are reluctant to highlight the negatives of NYAY as any word uttered against NYAY is likely to be interpreted as a criticism against the proposal for 'Minimum Income Guarantee' which is a noble concept.

Really, there is a case for expanding several schemes like the Employment Guarantee Schemes already in operation and putting together a comprehensive scheme, if possible, outside the government budgets, having the following features:

i. Target beneficiaries should be those who are in the employable age group (say, 20 to 60 years) considering all skilled/unskilled jobs for which they will be available on call, not presently availing the benefits of existing statutory schemes for social security. They can be asked to register with Employment Exchanges or at Special Employment Desks created for the purpose in offices of Municipal Corporations or other Local Self Government Offices.

ii. The payment should be to unemployed members of families which have no earning members with income over a pre-decided threshold limit and limited to the real gap between the threshold level and the actual.

iii. The funding could be from a corpus created by contributions from prospective employers who will benefit from the skill development initiatives and the availability of candidates with identified skills. While employment is provided through the scheme, a fixed percentage of the wages matched by an equal contribution from the employer could be retained for post-job social security of the beneficiaries.

iv. Care should be taken to ensure that even where employment assurance schemes are implemented, the compensations should be realistic.

Nyunatam Aay Yojana (NYAY)

NYAY was more of an election slogan came out clearly in a short article by Bhalchandra Mungekar, published in The Hindu Business Line (April 13, 2019). Mungekar is a former member of the Planning

Commission and Rajya Sabha and was also a member of the Congress Party's manifesto committee. The NYAY included in the Congress manifesto for 2019 Election assures 5 crore poorest families covering 25 crore people a guaranteed minimum income of Rs. 6000 per month or Rs. 72,000 per year. The assumption, according to Mungekar was that even the poorest family will have a monthly average income of Rs. 6000 and would need only additional Rs. 6000 for the target minimum monthly income of Rs. 12,000. Several options discussed by him in the article confirms one's fear that before inclusion of NYAY, no thought appears to have been given about raising the resources.

Universal Basic Minimum Income

Article 39 of the Indian Constitution mentions certain principles of policy to be followed by the State, including providing an adequate means of livelihood for all citizens, equal pay for equal work for men and women, proper working conditions, reduction of concentration of wealth and means of production from the hands of a few, and distribution of community resources to 'subserve the common good,' Constitutional objectives of building an egalitarian social order and establishing a Welfare State by bringing about a social revolution assisted by the State and have been used to support the nationalization of mineral resources as well as public utilities. Further, several legislations pertaining to agrarian reforms and land tenure have been enacted by central and state governments, in order to ensure equitable distribution of land resources.

It was in this context that during 2016, NITI Ayog mooted the proposal to accept Universal Basic Income (UBI) as one of the themes for the Economic Survey 2016–17 which was perceived as an effort to pursue further the spirit of the directive principles of state policy and re-dedicate budget exercise as a tool for ensuring distributive justice, which is a responsibility emanating from the constitutional provisions.

As a healthy debate on NYAY picks up, the various components of the concept of UBI, adequacy of the present levels of minimum wage, the path towards 'living wage,' the relationship between wage and savings, savings and social security, wage and healthcare and education expenditure in low income groups, factoring in the component of expenses for post-job life (pension in the case of regular jobs in the organized sector) in remuneration structure and so on will surface.

So far, discussions on such issues were isolated or confined to academia or research papers and committee reports. For India, once the political leadership gets convinced about the need for a realistic UBI, resources will not be a problem.

Writing about UBI in November 2016 in Moneylife, I had expressed the fear that "One possibility is, some vested interests will hijack proposal of UBI to mix it with "unemployment dole," an unhealthy practice existing in developed countries." With the floating of the idea of NYAY seriously by a major political party, this fear may come true.

Ground Level Realities

There are several pockets in India, including many in states like Kerala, where local population has successfully eliminated poverty and shown encouraging improvement with regard to crucial human development indicators. Attribute it to militant trade unionism or the color of the flags held by parties in power. The credit for this really goes to the insistence by enlightened workforce for a minimum basic wage. Hopefully, the concept of Universal Basic Minimum Income, as the debate picks up, will result in healthy deliberations on the need for grassroots level improvements in income distribution to ensure sustainable economic growth. A pragmatic approach to sharing of wealth can reduce several security concerns world over and ensure better living conditions, not only for the deprived class, but for many from the rich and the powerful who feel insecure today.

The Concept of Minimum Wage

Writing in The Hindu on September 1, 2016, author and renowned journalist G Sampath raised the question, "Do we need a minimum wage law?." He went on to explain the concepts of living wage, fair wage and minimum wage and debated the seriousness with which stakeholders are approaching these concepts. One has to concede that it is a farce to retain the concept of minimum wage which does not ensure an income for the worker (who works full-time) which helps him and his dependents survive with some savings left for the family's social security needs. The present levels of minimum wages vary across geographies and are not realistic. They do not reach anywhere near the cost of 5 components mandated by the 15th Indian Labour Conference (1957) which were:

i. The wage must support three consumption units (individuals)

ii. Food requirements of 2,700 calories per day

iii. Clothing requirements of 72 yards per year per worker's family

iv. Rent for housing area similar to that provided under the subsidised housing scheme and

v. Fuel, lighting and miscellaneous items of expenditure to constitute 20 per cent of the minimum wage.

It may be recalled that the Seventh Pay Commission had fixed minimum wage for central government employees at Rs. 18,000.

Viewed in the above context, GOI will have to concede at some stage the demand for some reasonable relativity for wages of the workers in the unorganized sector with the entitlements of workers in the organized sector having comparable responsibilities. Whenever specific issues relating to job security and compensation are raised by the unions or external agencies in the context of human development indicators in India showing uncomfortably low levels in comparison with similarly placed developing countries, some sporadic initiatives are taken by Centre or state governments. A comprehensive legislation covering all aspects of service in the unorganized sector is the need of the hour. Let us answer Sampath's brief question "Do we need a minimum wage law?," in the affirmative, as we need it to know the extent of aberrations and violations and for further refinements to think of a 'living wage' at the appropriate time. During 20th Century, we used Railway Time Tables to know the number of hours by which some trains were running late!

Time is opportune to revisit the prices, wages and income policy. If we do not do this, labour migration issues within the country and flight of skills and expertise from India may rise to unmanageable levels giving rise to several social problems. The revamp of prices, wages and income policy need to be done quickly and for making the processes transparent and findings and subsequent action plans acceptable for the stakeholders, there should be meaningful debates in legislatures and with users of services of workers.

Simmering discontent in the workforce emanating from the feeling that there is exploitation by the users of services, taking advantage of the helplessness of the workers, affect productivity and can have long term negative impact on economic growth. Sooner the governments and corporates amend the present approach, the better for the country.

Privatizing Public Sector

Srinivas Dindi, in his short but thought-provoking piece "Why privatize banks?" (Business Line, March 8, 2018) covered several aspects which do not justify further privatization of banking business in India at this juncture.

Let us concede that in India, since Nehruvian days, when 'public sector' commanded much more respect than today, there has been dissenting voices out to discredit public sector undertakings by any means available. We have witnessed the fall of reputed institutions like Unit Trust of India.

Legal hurdles in parity in functional matters with the private sector, weaknesses in top management caused by external interference in top-level appointments and HR issues using Government's ownership rights and sometimes caused by infiltration of people of doubtful integrity at higher levels, all contributed to the fall of public sector institutions.

As regards banking in India, as the source of funds and the clientele served by the public sector and private sector banks are the same, there should not have been much difficulty in providing a level playing field for both categories of banks.

But, in reality, only the private sector banks enjoyed functional autonomy to do business on their own terms (choice of clientele, freedom to operate where they want, less interference in HR-related matters including top-level remunerations and so on) within the overall contours of legislative restrictions.

Public sector banks are made answerable to their masters in Finance Ministry, accept responsibility for providing credit for all government-sponsored programs and ensure G-Secs are fully subscribed whenever central and state governments entered the market. Of course, in making government borrowings successful they have other public sector organizations like LIC which are expected to support the government on an ongoing basis.

By privatization, are we talking about handing over the banks to businessmen of doubtful integrity who run away with banks' funds? Or are we aiming at professionalization of Indian Banking System, irrespective of ownership? These are choices to be made fast.

Owner and Regulator

Sometime in 2019 "Check for fraud in Non-Performing Assets(NPAs) above Rs. 500 mn: Govt" was a headline in newspapers. On the face of it there is nothing extraordinary in 'owner' of a business giving operational instructions to the staff working under him. Government of India (GOI) as owner, has the responsibility to ensure smooth functioning of the Public Sector Banks (PSBs). Some recent developments have shaken the public trust in PSBs, which need to be restored quickly.

But in the given situation, the divergent instructions flowing from GOI and RBI confuse the already strained managements of PSBs. More likely, they will prefer waiting for instructions from Finance Ministry even after getting operational or supervision-related instructions from RBI, as it is the Finance Ministry which decides the fate of the top management in PSBs.

This is an embarrassing situation for the country's central bank which shoulders the responsibility of working under the Reserve Bank of India Act and administering Banking Regulation as legally mandated under the Act.

If GOI is not comfortable with the speed with which instructions are percolating down to banks from RBI, they should have a dialogue between them (GOI and RBI) and sort out issues. It is not in public interest for the two being seen talking differently and GOI sharing concerns in the media even before taking the banking regulator into confidence. Owner and Regulator have different kinds of responsibilities. Earlier this is conceded, the better for the image of the Indian Financial System which is already sagging. If banking gets affected by ego-related issues, the fall will be total and there will not be any public sector-private sector divide.

What Stalls PSBs Overhaul?

Who are preventing a wholesale overhaul of PSBs to bring them on par with the best among the world class commercial banks? They include the rich and the powerful who have substantial hold in governments in India, mainstream media houses and private sector business, who are more comfortable with laxity in appraisal of loan proposals and recovery arrangements in PSBs.

In the Punjab National Bank episode last decade, which triggered a series of debates, one could decipher the soft corner the lobbies against PSBs have for those who have looted the banks and brought disgrace to the Indian Banking System. The pressure on government to bring to books the people who swindled money is conspicuous by its absence. The effort has been to divert attention to procedural lapses or shift the responsibility from one shoulder to the other.

Why not build up a case for recovery from the borrowers, if necessary, by changing the laws? No, the motive is to shed tears for taxpayer or depositor while those who have looted banks get more time to hire better lawyers or idle away time till a change of government will help them out. Let us remember, these borrowers who account for a major portion of PSBs' NPAs have several pockets and only some of them are empty!

India's Gold Gets a Makeover

The caption is just an expression of a pious wish, but the prayers of 95 percent Indians who do not own more than 20 grams of gold per family are behind this thought, to make it happen. Perhaps India may be alone in the world to sustain the dubious distinction of grossly mismanaging an asset (read gold) the country has been holding for centuries in huge quantities, in multiple forms, and in various places. When the population starved and died as a consequence of bad governance or as victims of nature's wrath, Indian rulers allowed use of huge quantities of gold (a) to be wasted for gold-plating of roofs, flag-masts, and statues and (b) to be held in underground vaults, hidden and unaccounted, as unproductive 'assets.'

RBI's Gold Holdings

It has to be said to the credit of those who drafted Reserve Bank of India Act, 1934 which came into effect on April 1, 1935, that the framers of the Act included appropriate provisions in the Act to give the respect it deserved, to the yellow metal. Original Act provisions mandated RBI to ensure that 40 percent of the value of currency issued was backed by gold bullion and sterling reserves. Of course, with the higher level of trust of people in the central bank emerging, this was reduced and from 1956, RBI follows Minimum Reserve System (MRS). Under MRS, the central bank has to keep, a minimum reserve of Rs. 200 crore comprising of gold coin and gold bullion and foreign currencies. Out of the Rs. 200 crore, Rs. 115 crore should be in the form of gold coin and gold bullion.

Public trust in RBI is reinforced by a strong Balance Sheet maintained by the Reserve Bank of India.

When India faced a near crisis in meeting international payment obligations in 1991, it was the gold-holdings in the RBI's vault that came to the country's rescue. In January 1991, as India struggled to finance its essential imports, especially of oil and fertilizers, and to repay official debt, the Chandra Shekhar government knocked at different doors in the global financial system, which India considered friendly, for forex support. India, actually managed to get a bit of a breather with the first tranche of $755 million from the IMF, but that was too little.

By mid-March 1991 the global credit-rating agencies placed India on watch and by April, downgraded the country's sovereign rating from investment grade to a notch lower, making it virtually impossible to raise even short-term funds.

When all efforts to raise funds got stuck up with hurdles, some central banks and investment banks abroad pointed to the fact that India had enough gold which could be utilized.

Between July 4 and 18, 1991, the RBI pledged 46.91 tonnes of gold with the Bank of England and the Bank of Japan to raise $400 million. But as the economic situation improved, the government repurchased the gold before December the same year and transferred it to the RBI.

Memories, sometimes, haunt us at wrong occasions. Post-1947, UK and US and world bodies controlled by them and their allies were very friendly with India when they felt that we are able to manage our affairs on our own and kept a safe distance when we needed them most.

Hopefully, the time when other central banks and international bodies will be keeping their gold in the vaults of Reserve Bank of India can be a realizable dream during 2020's. That day, we will again remember 1991 with a smile.

After a long gap, RBI has added 208 tonnes of gold to the reserves during the last nine years. RBI purchased 200 tonnes of gold from the

International Monetary Fund (IMF), under the IMF's limited gold sales programme in 2009.

"This was done as part of the Reserve Bank's foreign exchange reserves management operations. The purchase was an official sector off-market transaction and was executed over a two week period during October 19–30, 2009 at market-based prices," the central bank announced on November 3, 2009. Again, after a gap of almost a decade, during 2017–18, RBI has added 8.46 metric tonnes of gold to the country's gold reserves taking the gold component in foreign exchange reserves to 566.23 metric tonnes. Even at this level, the gold component in the central bank's foreign exchange reserves constitutes only 6.3 percent. The US has the highest percentage of gold reserves with Fed Reserves at 74.9. See Table below:

World's top 10 central banks having a substantial gold component in their foreign exchange reserves (2017)

Serial No	Country	Gold Reserves (Tonnes)	As % to Forex Reserves
1	US	8133.5	74.9
2	Germany	3381	68.9
3	Italy	2451.8	68.0
4	France	2435.7	62.9
5	China	1797.5	2.2
6	Russia	1460.4	15
7	Switzerland	1040	6.7
8	Japan	765.2	2.4
9	Netherlands	612.5	61.2
10	India	557.7	6.3

After independence, India continued to spend huge amounts of precious foreign exchange to procure gold for meeting the ever-increasing demand from the domestic jewellery industry. In the recent past, GOI and RBI have taken several measures to restore the respectable position of the yellow metal, much beyond its decorative worth.

Errol D'Souza, Director, IIM, Ahmedabad in his note recorded in the 3rd Annual Report (2017–18) of the India Gold Policy Centre had this to say about gold management in India:

"As a macroeconomist, I uphold the view that integrating gold with India's broader economic vision is the touchstone for India's gold policy and gold markets. The foremost is adopting 'Make in India' policy which should address unexplored gold stocks below the ground, optimal use of gold stocks in circulation, and mobilize gold holdings held by individuals in lockers and temples."

Long back, someone had stated that India is a rich country with poor people. That person was not talking about the 'hidden wealth' in this country. In reality, the unaccounted wealth (for the time being the reference is not to tax evasion) in the custody of individuals and organizations in the form of gold, jewellery, and real estate, waiting to be mapped and mainstreamed must be worth trillions of rupees. If we are able to create a national consensus and build public trust to mainstream and pool a part of such domestic assets, India's dependence on external sources for our immediate development needs will come down drastically. This will be a challenge worth chasing.

It is not comforting to see 'fund mobilization drives' to help flood victims in Kerala at the instance of governments abroad being organized to provide financial support to India when our own wealth idle in vaults here. Fortunately, responding to media reports about an offer of 'aid' from a friendly kingdom (UAE), GOI was quick in advising Government of Kerala to politely decline such direct offers from foreign governments simultaneously clarifying that there was no ban on receiving contributions for relief and rehabilitation work from individuals and organizations of NRIs abroad.

The excerpts in Appendix I are from a media report about the Temple Treasure in Padmanabhaswamy Temple, Thiruvananthapuram.

Future Course

Reserve Bank of India should counsel GOI to understand the significance of the treasure in the form of gold stock with institutions and individuals lying idle in the country. As a short-term plan, concrete measures should be initiated for putting at least some 20 percent of the domestic gold stock to productive use in the next 5 years. This will reduce the country's gold import bill considerably. This can be achieved by:

- Making a realistic assessment of gold stock remaining idle in the country
- Providing incentives to holders of gold stock to properly account for the stock with them
- Making gold deposits with banks remunerative
- Introducing gold-backed financial instruments which are not dependent on imported gold (The tiny instruments now available in the form of Gold ETFs, gold coins and Sovereign Gold Bonds are indirectly dependent on import and have not attracted significant investor-interest)
- Quickly arrange for infrastructure, technology support and linkages for gold refining and certification facilities of international standard

RBI and GOI could consider even deficit financing for procurement of domestic gold as this could herald the emergence of a 'Golden Era' in the country's history.

Appendix I (Ref: India's Gold Gets a Makeover)

Temple Treasure in Padmanabhaswamy Temple, Thiruvananthapuram*

Inventory of the Treasure

The Supreme Court of India had ordered an amicus curiae appointed by it to prepare an inventory of the treasure. Full details of the inventory have not been revealed. However, newspaper reports gave an indication of some of the possible contents of the vaults. About 40 groups of objects were retrieved from Vault E and Vault F. Another 1469 groups of objects found in Vault C and 617 in Vault D. Over 1.02 lakh (102,000) groups of objects (referred to as articles collectively) were recovered from Vault A alone.

According to confirmed news reports, some of the items found include:

A 4-foot (1.2 m) high and 3-foot (0.91 m) wide solid pure-golden idol of Mahavishnu studded with diamonds and other fully precious stones.

A solid pure-golden throne, studded with hundreds of diamonds and precious stones, meant for the 18-foot (5.5 m) idol of the deity

Ceremonial attire for adorning the deity in the form of 16-part gold anki weighing almost 30 kilograms (66 lb)

An 18-foot (5.5 m) long pure-gold chain among thousands of pure-gold chains

A pure-gold sheaf weighing 500 kilograms (1,100 lb)

A 36-kilogram (79 lb) golden veil

1200 'Sarappalli' pure-gold coin-chains encrusted with precious stones weighing between 3.5 kg and 10.5 kg

Several sacks filled with golden artifacts, necklaces, diadems, diamonds, rubies, sapphires, emeralds, gemstones, and objects made of other precious metals

Gold coconut shells studded with rubies and emeralds

Several 18th-century Napoleonic-era coins

Hundreds of thousands of gold coins of the Roman Empire

An 800-kilogram (1,800 lb) hoard of gold coins dating to around 200 BC

According to varying reports, at least three if not many more, solid gold crowns all studded with diamonds and other precious stones

Hundreds of pure gold chairs

Thousands of gold pots

A 600-kg cache of gold coins from the medieval period

While the above list is on the basis of reports describing the July 2011 opening (and later) of Vaults A, C, D, E and F, a 1930s report from The Hindu mentions a granary-sized structure (within either of vaults C or D or E or F but not Vault A) almost filled with mostly gold and some silver coins. *A. Srivathsan (June 6, 2013)*. "When the vault was opened in 1931."

*Source: The Hindu Website

SECTION II – BANKING FOR ECONOMIC RECOVERY & GROWTH

RBI's Role as Confidence booster

Restoring trust: India's 2020's challenge

Focus shifts to growth at RBI

Multiple objectives, one policy

RBI's functional freedom

Reserve Bank of India: What lies ahead?

India's central bank: Challenges galore I

India's central bank: Challenges galore II

Reserve Bank's policy perceptions I

Reserve Bank's policy perceptions II

Rating RBI's policy: Beyond rate cuts

Monetary Policy I: In the right direction

Monetary Policy II: RBI takes charge

RBI's Role as Confidence Booster

Remember the Demonetization days? Those were the days India's central bank shouldered all the blame for all wrong reasons. While RBI as an institution had not failed in its responsibilities, inept delegations by a Governor who had no adequate awareness about ground realities of Indian bureaucracy and political leadership during the preparatory days (February to August 2016) for the Note-Ban ended up in an apparent messing up in handling of post-November 8, 2016 (the date on which Prime Minister Narendra Modi announced the withdrawal of Legal Tender status of the currency notes of value Rs. 1000 and Rs. 500. Urjit Patel, the governor who succeeded Dr. Raghuram Rajan in September 2016 was also an outsider (not from the IAS or Indian Banking Sector) like his predecessor and had communication problems with bureaucracy and political leadership which eventually ended up in his untimely exit from RBI.

The above introductory is to focus on the background of the present leadership at RBI. By the time RBI Governor Dr. Urjit Patel abruptly expressed his intention to leave RBI on December 11, 2018, Prime Minister Narendra Modi had a clear grasp of the situation at Mint Road and could ensure continuity in functioning of the central bank by sending a new governor there within 24 hours. The choice narrowed down on Shaktikanta Das as he had already proved his ability to handle tricky situations and his tactfulness to get along people and identify talent was no secret. We saw it in the limelight during the weeks that followed demonetization.

After taking over as governor, till date, insiders in RBI have several instances to quote when Das led the central bank team from the front, without himself claiming any credit for himself. He gave the whole credit to the team he led. His handling of two issues need special mention. One, the reserves controversy. By openly expressing opinions about transfer of RBI's reserves to GOI, top policy makers had embarrassed RBI which at one stage expedited the exit of Dr. Urjit Patel and later saw his Deputy's (Dr. Viral Acharya) resignation. With unreserved support from Shaktikanta Das RBI could appoint a panel with former governor Dr. Bimal Jalan as chairman and among others former Deputy Governor Dr. Rakesh Mohan as member to study the adequacy of reserves and the manner in which future RBI surplus income was to be appropriated. The Jalan Panel managed to come up with an excellent report on RBI's internal reserves management which was accepted by RBI for implementation. Another internal issue which was solved by Das was a long pending pension revision issue which was being dodged by finance ministry for almost two decades. Governor found out a via media of giving some temporary relief to the pensioners which incidentally boosted staff morale.

COVID19 Impact

After the medical fraternity, RBI was one of the major institutional participants which gauged the possible hurdles the invasion of the COVID19 pandemic will bring with it affecting the smooth functioning of the nation's lifelines including the financial system. Quickly, the central bank constituted a fairly large 'Core Team' under the leadership of Governor Shaktikanta Das which started functioning with War-like cautions to ensure uninterrupted functioning of core central banking functions including currency management and timely policy interventions.

In a media interaction during the initial period of COVID 19 Lockdown, RBI Governor acknowledged that "the measures taken by RBI during the recent times were unprecedented and unconventional." He was referring to the direct and indirect liquidity, monetary policy and regulatory interventions to facilitate smooth functioning of financial institutions which are undeniably the bedrock of our economy.

RBI provided various forms of financial support including flow of credit to the most deserving segments of the economy which suffered most as the Lockdown entered third month. RBI's own perception is that the easing of financing conditions considerably has resulted in alleviating financial stress and reducing volatility in certain segments. Though there are signs of cautious and slow opening of economic activity in some regions and areas are visible in recent weeks, RBI's own perception is that return to normalcy ornear normalcy will depend on how quickly the COVID curve flattens out.

During the MPC meeting held in May 2020, RBI Governor Observed:

"The Reserve Bank has been proactively managing liquidity. Since the MPC statement of February 6, 2020 the Reserve Bank has announced liquidity augmenting measures of ₹9.42 lakh crore (4.6 per cent of GDP). Monetary transmission has continued to improve with the weighted average lending rate (WALR) on fresh rupee loans declining by 43 bps in March; the decrease since February 2019, when the current cycle of rate cut began, being 114 bps" (see Appendix II for the text of Governor's statement at MPC Meeting held during May 2020)

RBI's efforts have limitations emanating from the dependence on the ability of the financial system to manage flow of credit to various sectors and demand from government for funds. Viewed from this angle GOI's package of measures gets significance. The Rs. 20 lakh crore Atmanirbhar package announced by GOI on May 12, 2020 comprises several components announced in phases by Finance Minister Nirmala Sitharaman during third week of May 2020. The package works out to 10 percent of India's GDP, which is among the most substantial in the world after US (13% of GDP) and Japan (20% of GDP). They included:

- The package allowed states to increase their borrowing limit unconditionally by 0.5 percent of individual state's Gross State Domestic Product (GSDP)

- Around Rs. 40,000 crore increase in MGNREGA allocation, over and above the budgeted Rs. 61,500
- Free food-grains to poor and cash to poor women and elderly Rs. 1.7 lakh crore
- Liquidity driven measures (including cut in interest rates etc) aggregating Rs. 6.5 lakh crore

The comparison in monetary terms with measures initiated by other countries may not be rational as India has a federal and multi-layer governance and budgeting system.

More challenges will emerge as the COVID curve flattens and the economy gets back on to the growth path again as a consequence.

Appendix II (Ref: RBI's Role as Confidence Booster)

Excerpts from the minutes of the Monetary Policy Committee meeting held at RBI on May 20–22, 2020

Statement by Shri Shaktikanta Das

The impact of COVID-19 on the domestic economy has turned out to be far more severe than initially anticipated. Lockdowns across major economies have also severely impacted economic activity across the globe. In the April WEO, the IMF projected the global economy to contract sharply by 3.0 per cent in 2020. GDP data for Q1:2020 and more recent high frequency indicators emanating from major advanced and emerging market economies, however, suggest that the contraction in global growth could be even deeper.

Domestic economic activity has been impacted severely by two months of lockdown which was imposed to contain the spread of the COVID-19 pandemic and save human lives. High frequency indicators for March-April 2020 suggest a collapse of demand. Industrial output, measured by the index of industrial production (IIP) for March, which included only seven days of the nation-wide lockdown, contracted by 16.7 per cent. The contraction was spread across sectors, with manufacturing shrinking by 20.6 per cent and capital goods production by 35.6 per cent. Private consumption, which has been the bedrock of domestic demand, also plummeted with the production of consumer durables falling by 33.1 per cent in March 2020 and that of non-durables by 16.2 per cent.

Limited data that are available for April suggest a further shrinkage in demand. India's merchandise trade slumped in April 2020, with exports contracting by 60.3 per cent and imports by 58.6 per cent. While railway freight traffic shrank by 35.3 per cent in April, steel consumption declined by 90.9 per cent. PMI manufacturing and PMI services in April slipped to unprecedented levels of 27.4 and 5.4 respectively.

Bank credit growth continues to be tepid, suggesting weak demand. Non-food credit of scheduled commercial banks (SCBs) grew by 6.5 per cent (y-o-y) as on May 8, 2020 as compared with 13.0 per cent a year ago. During 2020–21 so far (up to May 8, 2020), however, banks' investment in commercial paper, shares, bonds and debentures increased by ₹66,757 crore as against a decline of ₹8,822 crore during the same period last year, reflecting the impact of targeted long term repo operations (TLTROs) of the Reserve Bank.

The only silver lining has been the agriculture sector – the summer sowing is progressing well. As on May 10, 2020, summer sowing of all crops in the country was much higher by 43.7 per cent (37.9 per cent for rice, 74.8 per cent for pulses and 29.3 per cent for oilseeds) over last year's acreage. The harvest of rabi crop is almost complete. The forecast of normal monsoon by the India Meteorological Department (IMD) augurs well for agriculture output and farm incomes.

On inflation, the headline consumer price index (CPI) for April 2020 was not available on account of nationwide lockdown. Among the major groups, for which indices were released, food group inflation edged up in April 2020 (to 8.6 per cent from 7.8 per cent in the previous month) due to a broad-based increase in inflation across the food sub-groups.

The Reserve Bank has been proactively managing liquidity. Since the MPC statement of February 6, 2020 the Reserve Bank has announced liquidity augmenting measures of ₹9.42 lakh crore (4.6 per cent of GDP). Monetary transmission has continued to improve with the weighted average lending rate (WALR) on fresh rupee loans declining by 43 bps in March; the decrease since February 2019, when the current cycle of rate cut began, being 114 bps.

Looking ahead, the growth outlook has deteriorated sharply. There is still uncertainty as to when the COVID curve will flatten. Even as the supply side is expected to ease gradually as the lockdown related restrictions are phased out, it is the demand side, which will continue to weigh heavily on economic activity for some time to come. The impact of the fiscal and contingent liability measures announced by the government on demand creation needs to be carefully watched. Quick implementation of various reform measures can also inject growth impulses into the Indian economy in the medium to long term. Economic activity, however, is expected to contract in the first half of the year before recovering gradually in the second half of 2020–21 on the back of various fiscal, monetary and liquidity measures undertaken in the recent period. Overall, the GDP growth in 2020–21 is estimated to remain in negative territory. The pace of recovery will be contingent upon the containment of the pandemic and how quickly social distancing/lockdown measures are phased out.

It has become challenging to assess the inflation outlook in the absence of complete information on CPI. Food inflation is expected to moderate in the coming months as transport impediments and supply lines get eased. This is also corroborated by data on 22 essential commodities released by the Department of Consumer Affairs, which show that prices of several food items have declined in this month so far from the April levels. The meltdown in demand is also likely to result in a significant easing of price pressures in core goods and services. Weak demand conditions in the presence of strong favourable base effects could result in headline inflation falling below the target rate during Q3 and Q4 of 2020–21.

Since the last off-cycle MPC meeting on March 27, 2020 macro-financial conditions have deteriorated rapidly. The fast evolving trade-offs between growth and inflation have underscored the need for intensifying the assessment of the macroeconomic outlook, and the preparedness to act pre-emptively to address the swiftly shifting underlying economic and financial conditions and what they portend for the path going forward. Delaying timely monetary policy response by two weeks, waiting for the bi-monthly MPC meeting schedule, could be costly and irreversible. In fact, such a delay in monetary policy action could potentially become a source of risk itself to the deteriorating growth outlook. Monetary policy is a rapid deployment instrument of public policy, and monetary authorities, forewarned by prescient assessment of the prevailing macroeconomic conditions, have to be nimble. It is in this context that the scheduled second bi-monthly meeting of the MPC was advanced from June 3 to 5, 2020 to May 20 to 22, 2020.

As pointed out in the foregoing paragraphs, the risks to growth have become far more severe than in our assessment at the end of March 2020. It is expected that this diagnosis will be validated by hard data over the next few months, even as the overall outlook continues to be highly uncertain. The key challenge for monetary policy at this stage is to resuscitate domestic demand to avoid any harmful effect on income and employment in the short run and potential growth over the medium term. For strengthening domestic demand, it is important to revive consumer and business confidence. The Government has already announced a variety of measures to provide economic support to various sectors of the economy and protect the interests of vulnerable sections of society. The Reserve Bank has also been proactively managing liquidity to ensure that funds flow to all productive sectors of the economy. RBI has also been easing monetary policy to reduce the cost of funds/capital to revive domestic demand. While all these measures should help support demand as and when the nation-wide lockdown is lifted, but given the enormity of a collapse in demand, the need is to move ahead full throttle to ease financing conditions further so as to revive consumption and revitalize investment. Since banks are the key players in financing consumption and investment, it is also imperative that they remain adequately capitalised. The benign inflation outlook that is expected for the second half of 2020–21, coupled with the rising probability of a sharper loss of growth momentum in the near-term, has provided us with more policy space to ease financial conditions further and stimulate growth. Since the outbreak of COVID-19, the MPC has voted for front-loading its actions. In view of the deteriorating outlook, it is critical to reinforce these actions in sync with the space provided by the underlying conditions.

In assessing the magnitude of policy space, it is important to take into account the weak growth momentum, the need for prioritising growth in view of the less risky inflation outlook, and the need to assure benign financial conditions ahead of the recovery taking hold so that confidence is sustained. Considering all these factors, a reduction in the policy rate by 40 basis points would be appropriate. Accordingly, I vote for reducing the policy repo rate by 40 basis points from 4.4 per cent to 4.0 per cent. I also vote for persevering with the accommodative stance of monetary policy. The RBI remains watchful and shall not hesitate to use any conventional and unconventional tool in its toolkit to revive the macro economy and preserve financial stability while adhering to the inflation target.

Restoring Trust: India's 2020's Challenge

They say, "Well begun, is half done!" What has happened to planning in India?

In the initial days of post-independence governance, planning was a word woven into the fabric of every economic development activity in this country. At various stages we heard about Five Year Plans at national level and state level, Planning Commission, Community Development Blocks, All India Rural Credit Survey, Rural Credit Review, Agricultural Credit Review Committee, different committees on financial sector reforms, Lead Bank Scheme and so on. I had concluded my article on Dr. Raghuram Rajan in The Global ANALYST (September 2013) with the following observations:

"As observed in the earlier part of this article, Rajan is a fast learner. One hopes, during his OSD (Officer on Special Duty) days in RBI from the second week of August, 2013, he had occasion to glance the following books:

1. History of the Reserve Bank of India Vol I
2. All India Rural Credit Survey
3. Review of the Indian Monetary System (Sukhmoy Chakrabarty)
4. Report of the Committee on Financial Sector Reforms (Narasimham Committee-II)

These will give Dr. Rajan a feel of the role played by RBI since its inception in the evolution of the financial system to meet the country-specific needs. A reading of these books will also tell one why the cut and paste FSLRC report is not finding favor inside RBI. To conclude, I must say, the appointment of Dr. Rajan has raised huge expectations. Can the new RBI Governor help the economy, besieged by a plethora of challenges including a weakening currency, burgeoning deficits, sluggish growth, runaway inflation, rising interest costs etc., regain momentum?

Well, only time will tell."

This quote is here to recall that we continue to face the same problems we faced during pre-Modi 1.0 days and for solutions, ironically, we may have to search out the same old time-tested prescriptions by experts who made diagnosis after feeling the pulse of the Indian context.

On August 15, 2014 in his maiden Independence Day speech from the ramparts of Red Fort, Prime Minister Narendra Modi announced that our Planning Commission was a house in disrepair beyond renovation and he intended to dismantle it and rebuild a new structure (see Appendix III for excerpts). In reality, as on that day, the spirit of his message was applicable to the entire institutional structure supporting governance. Courts had accumulated pendency of over 30 million cases across the country at different levels, a report had been put together (Financial Sector Legislative Reforms Commission) for reforming the financial sector and the federal structure itself was showing signs of weaknesses for reasons including the pulls and pushes of the multi-party coalition politics that had become the order of the day.

During the four decades that followed independence, India had correctly understood the role of public sector organizations and the financial sector in economic development.

In his second book published post-retirement, titled "Rethinking Good Governance: Holding to Account India's Public Institutions," former CAG Vinod Rai, referring to the onslaught suffered by several constitutional bodies and statutory institutions in the recent past, observed that 'it goes to the credit of these robust institutions that they have managed to survive this onslaught. In the Epilogue to the book written after the 2019 Parliament Elections, referring to the public criticism of institutions like Election Commission of India, CAG, RBI and the Supreme Court, he observed:

"It has become the done-thing to attack institutions simply for performing their duty!"

But it goes to the credit of these robust institutions that they have managed to survive the onslaught. It needs to be recognized by politicians, as well as citizens, that governance is best served by allowing institutions the autonomy and independence mandated for them. It also needs to be recognized by the political executive that these institutions have been created by them, and the autonomy vested in them is by the legislature itself.

The tendency of any government that comes to power is to appoint its so-called 'confidants' to head the institutions, in the anticipation that they will toe the government's line. However, the experience has been that once in the chair, the appointees have invariably maintained the sanctity of the institution, displaying the professional integrity required of them. In fact, repeated attempts to cramp their functioning have met with a push-back."

Recently, Shri C V Subbaraman, a former central banker during an interaction, made the following observations about the current controversies on economic slowdown:

"All celebrated economists are good theorists. They can win many laurels, international rewards and recognitions for their "knowledge in the field of economy," even Nobel Prize. I understand that Nobel prize has never been missed in any year by economists from the start of Nobel Prize! Yet, with economists pedagoguing across the world with their often "I told you so" statements, the economy of the world has not found permanent solutions for many of the basic problems faced by humanity during the recent decades. There is an army of Economists world over, who keep giving fortuitous advice or indulge in opportunistic criticism of the handling of the economy by the powers that be. Here at home, everyone blames two factors for all ills in the system: Demonetization and "hasty" implementation of GST. Both the measures needed institutional and government support at the stage of implementation which was not forthcoming in adequate measure for reasons attributable to political views and lobbying by vested interests. True, regulatory measures to channelize financial transactions transparently and bring accountability in funds flow and management of resources affected "the informal economy." What is informal economy? It is the unregulated and unprotected employment and production sectors. Those who criticize demonetization and GST need to come forward with their position on black money and tax evasion.

Of late, there is a tendency on the part of senior bureaucrats and celebrity economists who occupy top positions in government and institutions in India to do what they want to do while in service and criticize the very organizations they served, once they retire."

Subbaraman's above observation was also in response to the averments in the media, like the following made by Maitreesh Ghatak:

"This (slowdown in the economic growth) is largely due to self-inflicted blows. The misguided shock therapy of demonetization delivered a massive shock and little therapy. In principle, the GST was a good idea, but it was implemented in a hasty, chaotic, and ham-handed way, like surgery without anesthetic. All this was done with the deeply misguided vision of converting a largely informal economy to a formal one overnight through diktat. All it did was simply dry up the informal sector, where nearly 80 per cent of the population is engaged, leading to massive losses in employment and income not fully captured by the GDP."

Agreed, we cannot brush aside concerns about economic growth slowdown. Rising consumption rates, falling household savings rate and high unemployment rate are all health issues affecting the Indian economy today. Comparisons with worse off nations or our own historic data do not comfort us. Those who are in charge of policy formulation are aware of the seriousness of the situation. RBI governor Shaktikanta Das went on record saying that "the weakening of private consumption, which for long has been the bedrock of aggregate demand, in particular, is a matter of concern. Private investment has also lost traction, with the corporate sector reluctant to make fresh investment" at the October

2019 Monetary Policy Committee meeting. He didn't conceal his concern and said:

"Economic activity has weakened further since the last MPC meeting in August 2019 with growth for Q1:2019–20 turning out to be 5 per cent. Various high frequency indicators show that economic activity remained weak in Q2. Inflation has evolved broadly along the projected lines and remains benign; while food inflation has edged up further in the last two months reflecting the sharper than expected increase in food prices, CPI inflation excluding food and fuel has moderated consistent with the slowing down of the economy."

These observations become relevant in the context of economists, analysts and those responsible for policy formulation and policy implementation at various levels in the hierarchy of governance searching for solutions for 21st Century problems using 20th Century tools. What is missing is a realistic assessment of India's own country-specific strengths, weaknesses, opportunities and threats.

Our Strengths Include:

- A strong democratic system of governance which is capable of absorbing occasional internal and external shocks. Whatever be the criticism, for India, change in governments has never affected continuity in governance.

- An assets-base accumulated from the past prudence and planning waiting to be mainstreamed and exploited. This include domestic savings idling in household lockers as jewellery and gold, temple/religious institutions' treasures, unutilized real estate properties, underutilized production capacities and uncultivated/under-cultivated land.

- Under-utilized talent and skill which also migrate to other countries for want of domestic opportunities.

If allowed to function within the existing mandates, we have a well-developed institutional system which can exploit the above strengths to reverse the temporary economic slowdown fast. What is lacking is the political will to guide the governmental machinery including legislatures and the institutions including judiciary, statutory bodies and the organizations/establishments in the public and private sector sectors to their optimum level of efficiency.

Unless trust is restored in the government and its various limbs, productivity of all resources including human resources will get affected and all talks of reforms and revival will remain on paper.

A National Balance Sheet

On October 23, 2019, Business Standard editorial captioned "The pension deficit" inter alia observed:

"The government tends to postpone expenditure to the extent possible and this is not restricted to one particular area. This practice must end because it doesn't help achieve anything"

Viewed in the context of recent developments, this is a revealing statement referring to the delay in payment of overdue National Pension System (NPS) contribution to PFRDA by GOI and needs immediate attention of all who have anything to do with finance in India. The introduction of National Pension System (Originally New Pension Scheme, December 2003) itself has an accounting jugglery background. When government pension schemes were following a "Pay As You Go" accounting practice and unfunded liability of such schemes rose to lakhs of crores of rupees, which attracted criticism, GOI discontinued defined benefit pension scheme for its employees (except defense personnel) prospectively and introduced NPS.

For decades now, Centre and state governments have been manipulating fiscal deficit figures with immunity by postponing payments due and receiving advance payments from organizations like RBI. Recently someone referred to such practices as "Borrowing from your grandchildren." Diverting funds under direction from institutions like LIC and delaying payments to statutory bodies and PSUs have become the order of the day. GOI and state governments need to think of a one-time cleansing of the "National Balance Sheet" by obtaining legislative approval for a higher fiscal deficit, if that is what obstructs facing reality.. Transparency in accounting will boost institutional morale leading to rise in public trust in the government and the financial system. A welcome byproduct will be rise in domestic/household savings and their mainstreaming.

The negative impact of a higher national level fiscal deficit can be got over by preparing and publishing a national balance sheet accounting for the entire domestic assets and liabilities held with government, corporates, individuals and all organizations.

A Case Study in Restoring Trust

The 2019 failure of the Punjab Maharashtra Cooperative Bank (PMC Bank) is an example of inefficient functioning of institutional system owing to inefficiency in enforcement of regulations and delayed administration of justice.

The depositor of the PMC Bank and common man in his capacity as a saver who deposits money in any bank in India may be concerned with the following issues:

- There is a Deposit Insurance and Credit Guarantee Corporation(DICGC) providing an insurance cover of upto Rs. one lakh (since revised to Rs. 5lakhs) per account-holder. It didn't provide any support when account-holders who had balances in current and savings accounts with PMC Bank were told that their deposits were frozen for six months and the maximum amount that can be withdrawn during the next six months was Rs. 1000/- (In subsequent days, in stages this limit was being revised upwards. Some relook at the adequacy of deposit insurance cover also is happening).

- What is the role the Registrar of Cooperative Societies as the authority having control over administrative matters of the bank will play in such situations?

- To what extent the stipulations and monitoring of maintenance of cash reserves (under RBI Act or BR Act) and Statutory Liquidity Reserves (under B R Act) will safeguard the interests of stakeholders in such situations?

There are no ready answers to such questions. But one feels uncomfortable, when none of the safeguards and safety-valves work in an emergency. No, we cannot just blame the judiciary, statutory bodies or institutions for the chaos and forget this till next calamity happens. Somewhere a beginning has to be made. Let it be from PMC Bank experience. It is heartening to find that some regulatory changes are happening to strengthen the supervisory role of RBI in relation to cooperative banks.

PMC Bank has over 10,000 crores of rupees collected as deposits from thousands of depositors spread in 6 or 7 states. GOI, RBI and representatives of some state governments should sit together and analyze what went wrong in this case. If necessary, new laws should be enacted. If amendments will take care, they should be carried out. The purpose should be to make adequate recoveries to pay the depositors in full. After that, let the PMC Bank start afresh, if it wants to continue in business. Restoring trust will be an uphill task.

Appendix III (Ref: Restoring Trust: India's 2020's Challenge)

Excerpts from Prime Minister Narendra Modi's Independence Day Speech, 2014*

India's federal structure is more important today than in the last 60 years. To strengthen our federal structure, to make our federal structure vibrant, to take our federal structure as a heritage of development, a team of Chief Ministers and Prime Minister should be there, a joint team of the Centre and the states should move forward, then to do this job, we will have to think about giving the Planning Commission a look. So, I am saying from the rampart of the Red Fort that it is a very old system and it will have to be rejuvenated, it will have to be changed a lot. Sometimes it costs more to repair the old house, but, it gives us no satisfaction. Thereafter, we have a feeling that it would be better to construct a new house altogether and therefore within a short period, we will replace the planning commission with a new institution having a new design and structure, a new body, a new soul, a new thinking, a new direction, a new faith towards forging a new direction to lead the country based on creative thinking, public-private partnership, optimum utilization of resources, utilization of youth power of the nation, to promote the aspirations of state governments seeking development, to empower the state governments and to empower the federal structure. Very shortly, we are about to move in a direction when this institute would be functioning in place of Planning Commission.

*Source: RBI

Focus Shifts to Growth at RBI

Madhusudhanan S concluded his article on Monetary Policy Committee published in June, 2019 issue of The Global ANALYST, with this observation: "The MPC should not only look at inflation targeting as its only goal, but it should also use its Monetary Policy Framework to accommodate policy to ensure sustainable growth. As it is said, 'Policy is meant for growth and not for impairment.'"

The above observation was recorded much before the MPC met between June 4 and 6, 2019 and RBI came out with a cut in base rate by 25 basis points simultaneously changing central bank's policy stance from 'neutral' to 'accommodative.' Just thought it appropriate to place on record that the time lag between analysts' perceptions and policy action by the central bank is reducing.

In India, at least since 1990's GOI and RBI have reconciled to the reality that fiscal and monetary policies are married with no option for a divorce. RBI has never asserted supremacy of monetary policy over the economic policy expectations of GOI. If there were visible frictions in their relationship, they emanated from the poor understanding on the part of certain individuals, of **the roles of GOI represented by the finance ministry and the RBI, the** institution responsible to implement certain mandated responsibilities.

The Monetary Policy Committee which has now been institutionalized by amending the RBI Act in reality is just a formalization of the role assigned to it by the Preamble of RBI Act, which has been played reasonably well by RBI, all along.

The clarity in the institutional mind of RBI as regards the objective of monetary policy and price stability comes out in uncertain terms in the then governor Dr. C Rangarajan's observations on the objectives of monetary policy and price stability in relation to the economy of India at the Second Conference of the Econometric Society's Regional Chapter for India and South Asia in Delhi on December 28, 1996 (see Appendix IV).

Monetary Policy Continuity

The policy perception of RBI has maintained continuity, despite the relatively short term natures of appointments at top level. This is evident from the observations made by Dr. Raghuram Rajan, who was governor during 2013–16, in a speech delivered at the Tata Institute of Fundamental Research (TIFR) on June 20, 2016 (almost 20 years after Dr. Rangarajan's speech quoted above). He said:

"The received wisdom in monetary economics today is therefore that a central bank serves the country and the cause of growth best by keeping inflation low and stable around the target it is given by the government. This contrast with the earlier prevailing view in economics that by pumping up demand through dramatic interest rate cuts, the central bank could generate sustained growth, albeit with some inflation. That view proved hopelessly optimistic about the powers of the central bank.

Put differently, when people say, 'Inflation is low, you can now turn to stimulating growth,' they really do not understand that these are two sides of the same coin. The RBI always sets the policy rate as low as it can, consistent with meeting its inflation objective. Indeed, the fact that inflation is fairly close to the upper bound of our target zone today suggests we have not been overly hawkish, and were wise to disregard advice in the past to cut more deeply. If a critic believes interest rates are excessively high, he either has to argue the government-set inflation target should be higher than it is today, or that the RBI is excessively pessimistic about the path of future inflation. He cannot have it both ways, want lower inflation as well as lower policy rates.

At the same time, the RBI does not focus on inflation to the exclusion of growth. If inflation rises sharply, for instance, because of a sharp rise in the price of oil, it would not be sensible for a central bank to bring inflation within its target band immediately by raising interest rates so high as to kill all economic activity. Instead, it makes sense to bring inflation back under control over the medium term, that is, the next two years or so, by raising rates steadily to the point where the bank thinks it would be enough to bring inflation back within the target range… More generally, the extended glide path over which we are bringing inflation in check appropriately balances inflation and the need for reasonable growth."

The emphasis, obviously is on the policy continuity at RBI with focus on price stability and growth, over decades, despite all constraints and pressures from various stakeholders.

The confidence with which RBI is moving forward simultaneously on policy front and in prompt initiation of regulatory and supervisory measures is building trust in those who are managing the institutional system in the financial sector. The central bank has, as expected, taken in its stride the pressures from policy makers in Delhi and those who are affected by its more stringent supervisory and regulatory stance to discipline players in the economy who are reluctant to fall in line. The message is, the RBI is willing to act decisively where warranted.

June 6, 2019 Policy Announcement

While Announcing the Bimonthly Monetary Policy on June 6, 2019, RBI Observed:

"The MPC notes that growth impulses have weakened significantly as reflected in a further widening of the output gap compared to the April 2019 policy. A sharp slowdown in investment activity along with a continuing moderation in private consumption growth is a matter of concern. The headline inflation trajectory remains below the target mandated to the MPC even after taking into account the expected transmission of the past two policy rate cuts. Hence, there is scope for the MPC to accommodate growth concerns by supporting efforts to boost aggregate demand, and in particular, reinvigorate private investment activity, while remaining consistent with its flexible inflation targeting mandate.'

Governor's observation in the post-policy announcement interaction with the media that the 'decision is driven by growth concerns and inflation concerns in that order' says it all.

Transmission of Interest Rates

A change in base rate by itself doesn't mean much for the economy in the Indian context, as the banking system's dependence on RBI is not significant. So far, the message that a cut in base rate by, say, 25 basis points in base rate is an expression of expectation that banks will reduce lending and deposit rates by quarter percent or near-about has not gone down the line loud and clear. There are reasons for this. Banks are aware of this expectation. But there are market realities. Banks' term deposit rates have some relationship with government's own savings schemes like Provident Fund and National Savings Schemes. Savers expect a reasonably positive return on their savings, net of inflation. So, there are constraints in reducing deposit rates. Despite all these, there exists a case for reducing lending rates, by reducing the need for high margins. If margins have to come down, efficiency in fund management, recovery rate and overall discipline in the financial system should improve. Here, RBI will expect support from policy makers and judiciary.

Signals from Mint Road

RBI-watchers have started assessing the impact of the presence of the new governor Shaktikanta Das at RBI who has crossed the halfway through the contracted tenure of 3 years. The brief tenures destabilize such positions. Intuitively, I feel the tidings are positive and with Nirmala Sitharaman as Finance Minister, the decade-old uncertainties in the relationship between North Block and Mint Road will become a memory we can push into archives. One hopes, Shaktikanta Das doesn't face destabilization threats of the kind faced by his immediate predecessors.

The change in RBI's own monetary policy stance from 'neutral' to 'accommodative' can be considered as symbolic. The IAS grounding and cordial relationship with his erstwhile colleagues in the Finance Ministry are helping Shaktikanta Das in solving contentious issues amicably with GOI.

Review of February 12, 2018 Circular

By any yardstick, RBI's February 12, 2018 circular on handling loan defaults was a landmark in regulatory guidance from the central bank. When the matter reached Apex Court, while the authority of the RBI was not contested, the circular was set aside on legal/technical grounds. RBI deserves praise for coming out with a revised version of the circular fast, rectifying some of the irritants in the original circular. The modifications in instructions include more time for banks for completing certain processes, bringing down the need for the assent of creditors to 75% for restructuring plan, provided all creditors agree to restructuring in principle and discretion to lenders with regard to design and implementation of resolution plans.

The minutes of the MPC meeting held from June 3 to 6, 2019 has been published after a fortnight from the meeting, as has been the practice.

Media has been trying to speculate too much about variations in the views expressed by governor and deputy governor Acharya. Members of MPC are duty-bound to express their views frankly at meetings and we should be thankful to RBI for being factual while recording minutes. Despite Deputy Governor Viral Acharya's curt observation that 'In spite of my dilemma, I vote-albeit with some hesitation – to front load the policy rate cut from 6 percent to 5.75 percent,' overall mood of the MPC is not apologetic about the cut and there seems to be no need for negativism on that count.

Having said that, one would like to read more into Michael Patra's following observation:

"Monetary policy by itself cannot bring about a reinvigoration of economic activity. Monetary policy is taking the lead as the first line of defence, but a coordinated full throttle effort by all arms of macroeconomic management is the need of the hour."

One hopes, the Finance Minister accepts this as a direct plea from RBI for fiscal policy support for achieving the results of the changed policy stance of the central bank, which includes accelerating economic growth. For the purpose, FM may have to tap the large non-traditional resources base of the country waiting to be exploited. Illustratively, accumulated wealth in the form of real estate, domestic gold-stock, external investments including those from NRIs and monetized wealth including agricultural income. Though moving away from the tradition of drawing from captive sources like disinvestment and asking PSUs and statutory bodies to cough up extra dividends or divert surpluses under guidance may be an uneasy option, it is a challenge worth accepting.

Appendix IV (Ref: Focus Shifts to Growth at RBI)

Excerpts* from the then RBI Governor Dr. C Rangarajan's observations on the objectives of monetary policy and price stability in relation to the economy of India at the Second Conference of the Econometric Society's Regional Chapter for India and South Asia in Delhi on 28/12/96.

I would like to take this opportunity given to me this morning to raise one issue in monetary policy that still remains contentious despite overwhelming agreement among policy makers in industrially advanced countries. The issue relates to the objective of monetary policy. The question is: What should be the objective or objectives of monetary policy and whether in the Indian context, maintenance of price stability should be the dominant objective of monetary policy?

The issue of objective has become important because of the need to provide clear guidance to monetary policy makers. Indeed this aspect has assumed added significance in the context of the increasing stress on autonomy of central banks. While autonomy has to go with accountability, accountability itself requires a clear enunciation of goals.

Monetary policy has now moved to the centre stage of economic policy-making the world over. In the 1930s and in the first two decades after the Second World War, monetary policy was relegated to the background. The ascendancy of fiscal policy during this period was due in part to the depression of the 1930s, and the process of reconstruction immediately after the Second World War and the acceptance of the Keynesian dictum that fiscal action was necessary to prevent deficiency in the aggregate demand. However, the 1970s saw the emergence of a combination of high inflation and low growth – 'stagnation' as it came to be called – and the standard Keynesian analysis was hard put to explain that phenomenon. Consequently, monetary policy re-emerged as an instrument of economic policy particularly in the fight against inflation. Issues relating to the conduct of monetary policy came to the forefront of policy debates in the 1980s. The relative importance of growth and price stability as the objective of monetary policy as well as the appropriate intermediate target of monetary policy became the focus of attention. Over the years, a consensus has emerged among the industrially advanced countries that the dominant objective of monetary policy should be price stability.

Incorporation of this objective in the Maastrischt Treaty is indeed a reflection of this consensus. Differences however, exist among central banks even in industrially advanced countries as regards the appropriate intermediate target. While some central banks consider monetary aggregates and therefore monetary targeting as operationally meaningful, some others focus exclusively on interest rate even though the inter-relationship between the two targets is well recognized.

A similar trend regarding monetary policy is discernible in developing economies as well. Much of the early literature on development economics focused on real factors such as savings, investment and technology as main springs of growth. Very little attention was paid to the financial system as a contributory factor to economic growth. In fact, many writers felt that inflation was endemic in the process of economic growth and it was accordingly treated more as a consequence of structural imbalance than as a monetary phenomenon. However, with the accumulated evidence, it became clear that any process of economic growth in which monetary expansion was disregarded also led to inflationary pressures with a consequent impact on economic growth. Accordingly, importance of price stability and therefore the need to use monetary policy for that purpose also assumed importance in developing economies. Nonetheless, the debate on the extent to which price stability should be deemed to be the over-riding objective of monetary policy in such economies continues.

Monetary policy is an arm of economic policy and in that sense, the objectives of monetary policy are no different from the overall objectives of economic policy. The broad objectives of monetary policy in India have been

    a. to regulate monetary expansion so as to maintain a reasonable degree of price stability; and

    b. to ensure adequate expansion in credit to assist economic growth.

The emphasis between the two objectives has changed from year to year depending upon the conditions prevailing in that and the previous year.

The question of a dominant objective arises essentially in view of the multiplicity of objectives and the inherent conflict among such objectives. Jan Tinbergen had argued decades ago that it was necessary to have at least one instrument for each target. In this regard, it must be recognized that certain objectives are better suited or more easily achieved with certain instruments than with others. This 'assignment rule' favours monetary policy as the most appropriate instrument to achieve the objective of price stability.

The crucial question that arises is whether the pursuit of the objective of price stability by monetary authorities undermines the ability of the economy to attain and sustain higher growth. A great deal of research effort has been spent on the examination of the trade-off between economic growth and price stability.

The well known Phillips curve showed that there was an inverse relationship between rate of change in wage rate and unemployment rate suggesting thereby a trade-off between inflation and unemployment. The original article of Prof. Phillips was published in 1958. The Phillips curve relationship has subsequently been challenged both from theoretical and empirical standpoints. The downward slope of the curve arises basically because of the presence of money illusion and expected inflation deviating from actual inflation.

At present the controversy is centred around the possible short-run and long-run 'trade-off' between inflation and unemployment. This distinction primarily stems from the assumption of 'error-learning' process in the determination of inflationary expectations – workers do have an anticipation on the inflation, but because they judge the inflation performance from the past data, the adjustment between the expected and actual inflation is slow. This implies that in the short-run, nominal wage rise will not fully absorb the actual inflation, and as such, it is argued, there is scope for reducing unemployment through inflation. As people adjust their expectations of inflation, the short-run Phillips curve shifts upward and the unemployment rate returns towards its 'natural' level. As the expected inflation catches up with actual inflation, the Phillips curve becomes vertical, denying thereby a 'trade-off' between

inflation and unemployment in the long run. The Phillips curve thus provides at best a temporary trade-off between inflation and unemployment when the economy is adjusting to shocks to

aggregate demand and as long as expected inflation is lower than actual inflation. The long-run Phillips curve becomes almost vertical at the natural rate of unemployment.

Of course, there is a possibility of lengthening the short-run 'trade-offs' indefinitely, since inflation surprises in each period can elongate the long-run perpetually. But, in that case the 'trade-offs' will become sharper in each successive period. In other words, to maintain the unemployment below the 'natural' rate, policy authorities will have to inflate the economy at higher rates in each successive period. This has a major policy implication even if the economy does not operate on the long-run vertical Phillips curve. Under the 'rational expectations hypothesis,' as there are no deviations between 'actual,' and 'expected' inflation, both in the short-run and long-run, Phillips curves are treated as being vertical with no trade-off between inflation and unemployment.

Another policy related question is the shape of the short-run Phillips curve itself. In the real world, wages and prices remain sticky, as employment contracts are fairly long and there is also a cost in changing the individual prices too often, or renegotiating wages each time after a price rise. As argued by Fischer (1994), the nature of stickiness in wages and prices could be different in different economies and this could also be a function of the inflation history of the country concerned. Countries with high inflation rates tend to find themselves on the steeper portion of the short-run Phillips curve than low inflation countries which are more likely to be on the flatter side. Therefore, 'trade-off' between price stability and employment or output even when it does exist, is sharper for countries with relatively high inflation rates than those with low inflation rates.

The case of price stability as the objective of monetary policy rests on the fact that volatility in prices creates uncertainty in decision making. Rising prices affect savings adversely while making speculative investments more attractive. The most important contribution of the financial system to an economy is its ability to augment savings and allocate resources more efficiently. A regime of rising prices vitiates the atmosphere for promotion of savings and allocation of investment. Apart from all of these, there is also a social dimension. Inflation affects adversely those who have no hedges against inflation and that includes all the poorer sections of the community. Of course, a critical question in this context is at what level of inflation the adverse consequences begin to set in.

Inflation affects fiscal balance in several ways. It adversely affects fiscal deficit when elasticity of expenditure to inflation is higher than that of revenue. A more significant impact of inflation arises from its effect on interest rate and the dynamic sustainability of the fiscal situation. High rates of inflation signal weak resolve to control inflation and imply higher expected inflation in future. This gives rise to upward rigidity in nominal interest and leads to high debt service burden on the budget, thus reducing the manoeuvrability of fiscal management.

It is well recognized that adverse implications of inflation are higher at high rates of inflation, while a moderate inflation rate could be manageable without implying severe costs. International evidence suggests that the costs of uncertainty tend to rise in a non-linear fashion with inflation rate exceeding a threshold. One important caveat in interpreting the threshold of inflation rate beyond which costs exceed benefit is the provision of inflation protection measures available in the economy, which tends to moderate the adverse implications to some extent. Countries with a moderate inflation rate but inadequate indexation provision may show a higher degree of sensitivity to inflation, than those with low inflation. Most of the industrialized countries in the recent years have moved into an inflation rate ranging between two to three per cent. Among the developing countries, some of the fast growing East-Asian economies have in recent years not only demonstrated low inflation rates ranging between three to five per cent, but the growth rate at these inflation rates has been fairly high at around eight per cent.

Empirical evidence on the relationship between the inflation and growth in cross-country frameworks is somewhat inconclusive because such studies include countries with inflation rate of as low as one to two per cent as well as countries with inflation rates going beyond 200 and 300 per cent. While a number of studies have concluded that the negative impact of inflation on growth is high at high rates of inflation, there is no consensus about the threshold inflation rate beyond which the negative impact becomes pronounced. A study by Bruno indicated that growth rates declined steeply as the inflation rate went beyond 25 per cent. Another study also based on cross section of countries reported that the negative effect of inflation was very pronounced and powerful at inflation rates exceeding eight per cent. What the appropriate inflation threshold beyond which costs tend to exceed benefits need to be estimated for each country separately. Nevertheless, people worry about even moderate inflation levels because if not held in check, a little inflation can lead to higher inflation and eventually affect growth.

A macro-econometric model of the Indian economy shows that a 10 per cent sustained increase in real public investment in non-agriculture sector, financed by money creation leads to an annual inflation rate of about 2.3 per cent and additional GDP growth of one percent, on an average, during the first two years, while in the span of 10 to 15 years, inflation rate rises to about 17 per cent per annum and additional output growth slows down considerably to average 2.7 per cent during this period. This implies that in the long run a sustained improvement in the growth scenario through monetary financing of the deficit could involve a severe trade-off in terms of inflation – every one per cent additional output growth implies nearly 6 to 6.5 per cent rise in inflation rate in the long run.

We, in India, need to have an appropriate fix on the acceptable level of inflation rate. In the 1970s, the average annual inflation rate as measured by the wholesale price index was nine per cent. In the 1980s, it was eight per cent. However, in the period between 1990 and 1995, the average inflation rate has remained around 10 per cent. The objective of the policy should be to keep the inflation rate around six per cent. This itself is much higher than what the industrial countries are aiming at and therefore will have some implications for the exchange rate of the rupee. Monetary growth should be so moderated that while meeting the objective of growth it does not push the inflation rate beyond six per cent.

A question that arises in this context is whether monetary policy by itself is able to contain inflationary pressures particularly in developing economies like ours. It is true that developing economies like India are subject to greater supply shocks than developed economies. Fluctuations in agricultural output have an important bearing on the price situation. Nevertheless, continuous increase in prices which is what inflation is about cannot occur unless it is sustained by a continuing increase in money supply. Control of the money supply has thus to play an important role in any scheme aimed at controlling inflation.

The controversy over the objective of monetary policy has reached such a pitch that some have described central bankism as a religion with hard money as supreme god and inflation as devil. Let me however say that the commitment to a reasonable degree of price stability is not a dogma. It is good economics.

*Source: BIS Review 8/1997(BIS Website)

Multiple Objectives, One Policy

"Gold's long-term prospect is up, up and up, and the reason why I say hat is money supply is up, up and up. I think you have to be buying at any level, frankly. With the efforts by the central banks to lower interest rates, they're going to be printing like crazy"

Mark Mobius, Founder, Mobius Capital Partners

(Quoted in Business Standard, August 21, 2019)

After absorbing a couple of shocks (Yes, the reference is to the controversial reference to Section 7 of RBI Act by finance ministry while communicating with the then governor Urjit Patel and the premature exits of Patel and Viral Acharya), quickly RBI returned to business as usual in December 2018-January 2019. The grace with which RBI handled the situation deserves appreciation. If someone is still in doubt about the relationship between RBI and GOI, at every opportunity available, the finance minister Nirmala Sitharaman has been trying to clear the air by asserting that the two are and will continue to be on the same page.

The statutorisation of the Monetary Policy Committee, has brought down considerably the instances of interventions from political leadership (read finance ministry) in the conduct of monetary policy by the central bank. GOI has also ensured that the MPC remained a body of professionals with continuity of incumbents.

RBI has all along been performing multiple roles in monetary policy formulation and supervisory functions, besides management of currency, debt and forex reserves with success within the constraints emanating from growth-related and fiscal policy considerations.

An Unconventional Rate Cut

As decided by the Monetary Policy Committee (MPC) which concluded its three-day meeting on August 7, 2019, RBI announced a repo rate cut by 35 basis points (one basis point is one hundredth of one percent), the highest in the recent past. The focus being on arresting the falling economic growth, RBI simultaneously insisted that banks must pass on the benefits to their customers.

The August 7, 2019 Resolution of the MPC Said:

"On the basis of an assessment of the current and evolving macroeconomic situation, the Monetary Policy Committee (MPC) at its meeting today decided to:

- reduce the policy repo rate under the liquidity adjustment facility (LAF) by 35 basis points (bps) from 5.75 per cent to 5.40 per cent with immediate effect.

  Consequently, the reverse repo rate under the LAF stands revised to 5.15 per cent, and the marginal standing facility (MSF) rate and the Bank Rate to 5.65 per cent.

- The MPC also decided to maintain the accommodative stance of monetary policy.

  These decisions are in consonance with the objective of achieving the medium-term target for consumer price index (CPI) inflation of 4 per cent within a band of +/−2 per cent, while supporting growth."

  The observation made by Governor Shaktikanta Das that "Given the current and evolving inflation and growth scenario at this juncture, it can no longer be a business-as-usual approach. The economy needs a larger push.," perhaps sums up the central bank's constraints and concerns (see Appendix V for governor's statement included in the minutes of MPC meeting published on August 21, 2019)

Transmission of Interest Rates

One is not sure why media and analysts are shy to disclose the truth that, of late, a change in base rate by itself doesn't mean much for the economy in the Indian context. This could be because the banking system's dependence for resources on RBI is not significant. But these are commonsense views which policy makers usually ignore. This time around, experts have similar views. This is what Madan Sabnavis, Chief Economist, CARE Ratings wrote in The Hindu Business Line on August 9, 2019:

"Since February there has now been a 110 bps reduction in the repo rate, of which, 75 bps came between February 7 and June 6. How have interest rates reacted? First, the weighted average interest rate on deposits came down from 6.91 per cent in January to 6.84 per cent in June. The weighted average lending rate (WALR) for fresh loans of all banks came down from 9.97 per cent to 9.68 per cent in June which is lower by 29 bps and hence a better response." He further observed that the repo cost *per se* will not matter as it is applicable to not more than 1 per cent of NDTL (net demand and time liabilities) which is permissible under LAF (liquidity adjustment facility).

So far, the message that a cut in base rate by, say, 25 basis point is an expression of expectation that banks will reduce lending and deposit rates by quarter percent or near-about, has not gone down the line loud and clear. There are reasons for this. Banks are aware of this expectation. But we cannot ignore market realities. Banks' term deposit rates have some relationship with government's own savings schemes like Provident Fund and National Savings Schemes. Savers expect a reasonably positive return on their savings, net of inflation. Till inflation starts flirting with zero or below, any reduction in retirement savings will mean a cut in the daily expenses of senior citizens. So, there are constraints in reducing deposit rates.

Despite all these, there exists a case for reducing lending rates, by reducing the need for high margins. If margins have to come down, efficiency in fund management, recovery rate and overall discipline in the financial system should improve. Here, RBI will expect support from policy makers and judiciary.

There are indications that some banks may accept the challenge of linking their deposit and lending rates to the central bank's base rate which may gradually earn some respectability for the repo rate.

Tenure Erosion

GOI's political preference while making top-level appointments has always been for amenable individuals. But merit and professional integrity were rarely compromised while filling top level positions in RBI. The reasons for Dr. Raghuram Rajan not getting extension beyond 3 years and Dr. Urjit Patel and Dr. Viral Acharya cutting short their own tenures as governor and deputy governor are 'personal' though not in the same sense the word is generally understood.

The three distinguished economists came to RBI on sort of 'sabbatical' retaining their liens elsewhere. One is not sure whether any other similar organization would have allowed its employees, at such levels, to keep a lien in another organization. Such inter-mobility of roles, for attracting talent, in the normal course, should have been 'outside' the regular rolls.

For appointments at the highest level in organizations like RBI and other establishments, GOI should maintain a live talent pool in a transparent manner from among willing candidates working anywhere in the world.

The Indian Administrative Service (IAS) officers, throughout their career, go through different types of challenges, most of which emanate from the conflict between their own social and educational background and those of their 'temporary' political bosses. Their comfort level improves only when they reach fairly senior levels, say Joint Secretary and above when they start to directly interact with policy makers and get an opportunity to contribute to policy-making.

Last 5 years have seen the Indian financial sector getting churned chaotically in unprecedented proportions. Contributing factors included diverse interests of depositors and borrowers, owners (including GOI) and supervisors and regulators (represented by RBI) and the short-term views on long-term policy issues taken by political leadership represented by GOI.

In banking industry which is dependent on deposits from public for bulk resources, the bifurcation of institutions into public and private sectors for the purpose of regulation and supervision as also social responsibilities is fallacious. Aspects like the quality of management and the level of specialization in serving the clientele should differentiate institution 'A' from institution 'B' in the eyes of the public who make informed choices.

Instead of thinking in terms of quick-fix solutions like recapitalization and privatization, GOI should fast-track consolidation and infusion of professionalism in running public sector banks. It is heartening to see that Finance Minister Nirmala Sitharaman has since announced Centre's decision to reorganize Public Sector Banks going by the spirit of the decades old Narasimham Committee recommendations.

The short tenures of Dr. Raghuram Rajan and Dr. Urjit Patel as governors and Dr. Viral Acharya as Deputy Governor at RBI in a way benefited policy makers in Delhi. They received unbiased opinions about the 'Do's and Don'ts' relating to the management of fiscal and monetary policies and supervision of institutions in the financial sector from independent celebrity economists who had no country-bias.

Facing Fiscal Reality

Ever since Economic Survey 2016 erroneously estimated the quantum of RBI's reserves inflating the figures by including fictitious revaluation reserves and 'unilaterally' suggested avenues for deployment of the assumed surplus, there have been clarifications and analyses including Dr. Raghuram Rajan's September 3, 2016 Delhi speech and Dr. Rakesh Mohan's three-part article published in October 2018 in a financial newspaper.

By forcing transfers from the reserves of the central bank, Centre may not be a net gainer, as the government may have to find takers for the securities/assets RBI may sell to monetize unrealized reserves. In the public eye, the balance sheet of RBI will become weak as the central bank's capital remains static at 5 crores of rupees and the balance sheet strength depends on its reserves in different 'pockets.'

In the fitness of things, statutory bodies should have functional freedom to manage their funds in a professional and transparent manner within the statutory provisions.

Financial Sector Regulation and Supervision

Writing in the Business Standard during July 2019, Professor T T Ram Mohan of IIM, Ahmedabad raised certain relevant questions on the duality of control over financial institutions including banks and NBFCs at ground level and answered them giving the evolution of regulatory and supervisory system in the Indian financial sector over the years.

Though there is no use lamenting over the omissions and commissions in past reports, for record's sake, mention has to be made about the tangent route the FSLRC (Financial Sector Legislative Reforms Commission) took, trying to reinvent the central bank and truncate its functional limbs.

The FSLRC failed to listen to professionals among its own members. The piecemeal approach to policy formulation affecting financial sector during the second half of the current decade is attributable to the diversion opted by FSLRC from its real mandate.

Having said that, there is no denying the fact that GOI and RBI have been deftly building the Institutional System in the financial sector to meet the changing needs. Setting up of IDBI, NABARD, NHB, SIDBI and Exim Bank at the apex level and coming into being of SBI, public sector banks, Regional Rural Banks and small banks should be seen in this perspective. The missing link is an HR initiative to ensure professionalism in the functioning of all these institutions. The RBI board decision "to create a specialized supervisory and regulatory cadre" should be perceived as a message for infusing professionalism at all levels in the financial sector. Reserve Bank's resolve to improve governance in the financial sector was evident in the speech delivered at the Annual Global Banking Conference in Mumbai on August 19, 2019 by RBI Governor Shaktikanta Das (Appendix VI)

RBI's Economic Capital Framework (ECF)

In the context of RBI's growing balance sheet size, the present level of the central bank's share capital and reserves is not huge. RBI has been using its funds for investment in shares of apex financial institutions and transferring divestment proceeds of such investments to GOI most of the time. By a conscious decision, RBI's share capital remains static at Rs. 5 crore since inception (1935). Time is opportune to amend the provisions of RBI Act to provide for raising the share capital of RBI to a decent level, say the equivalent of US $200 billion and to create specific enabling provisions to augment reserves out of surplus income, to a higher level than the present 5.5 to 6.5 percent of assets.

Making RBI Owner-Driven

Though there can be difference of views on scale, all along, those who occupied top positions in RBI, with the exception of a few, have risen to the responsibilities given to them and did not surrender their mind or freedom of expression for fear of North Block's displeasure. Governors like Dr. D Subbarao started speaking RBI language within months of their occupying the corner office at Mint Road. RBI is a lucky institution. The new finance minister is the new 'avatar' who will, by appropriate policy signals, save the image of RBI and send out a clear message that India's central bank is not facing the threat of extinction.

Unlike other organizations, continuity at the top is important for central banks. The normalization of the abnormality of short-term tenures for governors and his deputies in RBI from the beginning of the current decade has affected the efficient and smooth functioning of the organization. Centre failed to take cognizance of the mood of the NewGen incumbents who accept top positions in RBI. They are not coming depending on any political backing or for improving their CV for their next assignment. They enjoy 'doing central banking' as part of their professional advancement.

Delhi's attack on Mint Road started with the attempt to truncate RBI using the report of the Financial Sector Legislative Reforms

Commission as a sharp enough weapon. The timely arrival of Dr. Raghuram Rajan on the scene, who had a clear understanding of the evolution and role of RBI helped the institution remain in one piece. Another attack, the gravity of which was not gauged by Dr. Rajan, was to weaken the balance sheet of RBI.

We Need the RBI Alive

It may be just coincidence that the news "Viral Acharya quits RBI" (Business Standard, June 24, 2019) becomes a headline on a day the maiden article of the monthly column by former RBI governor Y V Reddy on "Whither central bank independence" gets published on another page in the newspaper. GOI has limited time left to save the image of RBI and send out a clear message that India's central bank is not facing the threat of annihilation, a fear expressed by S S Tarapore long back.

Unlike other organizations, continuity at the top is a must for central banks. The normalization of the abnormality of short-term tenures for the governor and his deputies in RBI from the beginning of the last decade has affected the efficient and smooth functioning of the organization. Centre failed to take cognizance of the mood of the incumbents who accepted top positions in RBI.

Appendix V (Ref: Multiple Objectives, One Policy)

Excerpts from the minutes of MPC Meeting held in August 2019

Statement by Shri Shaktikanta Das

Economic activity has shown signs of further weakening since the last MPC meeting in June 2019. Several high frequency indicators have either slowed down or contracted in recent months. Headline CPI inflation has evolved broadly along the projected lines; CPI inflation excluding food and fuel continued to soften, while food inflation has edged up. Global economic activity has been losing pace, weighed down by intensifying trade tensions and geo-political uncertainty. GDP numbers for Q2:2019 in respect of some major advanced and emerging market economies have been subdued. Central banks in both advanced and emerging market economies have been increasingly resorting to more accommodative stances of monetary policy.

Headline CPI inflation rose to 3.2 per cent in June 2019 from 3.0 per cent in April-May. Food inflation rose by 100 bps in May-June, driven mainly by a pick-up in prices of meat & fish, pulses and vegetables. On the other hand, CPI inflation excluding food and fuel moderated for the fourth consecutive month to 4.1 per cent in June, caused by a broad-based softening across groups, particularly clothing and footwear; household goods and services; and transport and communication. This reflects subdued input cost pressures relating to both agriculture and industrial raw materials and further weakening of domestic demand conditions. Inflation in the fuel and light group also decelerated in May-June, despite the uptick in liquified petroleum gas (LPG) prices. Inflation expectations of households in the July 2019 round of the Reserve Bank's survey moderated further by 20 basis points for the 1-year ahead horizon, though they remained unchanged for the 3-month ahead horizon. Cumulatively, inflation expectations of households have declined significantly by 180 basis points for the 3-month horizon and 190 basis points for the 1-year horizon in last five survey rounds. This suggests that inflation expectations of households are gradually getting better anchored. Overall, the inflation situation remains benign. CPI inflation has been projected at 3.1 per cent for Q2:2019–20 and 3.5–3.7 per cent for H2:2019–20, with risks evenly balanced. CPI inflation for Q1:2020–21 has been projected at 3.6 per cent.

Turning to economic activity, total area sown under kharif crops was 6.6 per cent lower as on August 2 than a year ago, with significant catching up taking place in recent weeks. Industrial activity continued to be weak in May 2019, impacted mainly by manufacturing and mining. In terms of use-based classification, growth of capital goods and consumer durables decelerated. However, growth of non-durables accelerated in May. The index of eight core industries decelerated in June. Merchandise exports and imports contracted in June. Seasonally adjusted capacity utilisation moderated to 74.5 per cent in Q4:2018–19 from 75.6 per cent in Q3. Based on early results of listed companies, demand conditions in the manufacturing sector remained weak in Q1:2019–20, with sales of manufacturing companies contracting by 2.4 per cent (y-o-y), caused mainly by petroleum, automobile and iron and steel companies. On the positive side, the Reserve Bank's business assessment index (BAI) for Q1:2019–20 improved marginally. The manufacturing PMI rose in July, supported by a pick-up in production, higher new orders and optimism on demand conditions in the year ahead.

Several high frequency indicators for May-June also suggest weakening of services sector activity. Two key indicators of rural demand, viz., tractor and motorcycle sales, continued to contract. Among indicators of urban demand, while passenger vehicle sales contracted in June, domestic air passenger traffic growth turned positive in June after three consecutive months of contraction. Two key indicators of construction activity, viz., cement production and steel consumption, also contracted/slowed down. Import of capital goods contracted in June, suggesting weakening of investment activity. The services PMI moved into expansion zone in July on increase in new business activity, new export orders and employment.

GDP growth for 2019–20 has been revised downwards from 7.0 per cent in the June policy to 6.9 per cent – in the range of 5.8–6.6 per cent for H1:2019–20 and 7.3–7.5 per cent for H2 – with some downside risks. GDP growth for Q1:2020–21 is projected at 7.4 per cent. The impact of monetary policy easing since February 2019 and favourable base effects are expected to support GDP growth, especially in the second half of the year.

Liquidity in the system has been in surplus since June 2019 with the surplus absorbed under the reverse repo window of the Reserve Bank being almost `2.0 lakh crore on August 6, 2019. The past policy rate cuts have been fully transmitted to financial markets. The weighted average lending rate (WALR) on fresh rupee loans of banks has declined by 29 bps during the current easing phase so far (February-June 2019). The transmission to bank lending rates has been inadequate, though it is expected to improve in the coming weeks and months. Credit growth has slowed down somewhat in the recent period; credit to micro, small and medium enterprises, in particular, remains anaemic.

Overall, there is clear evidence of domestic demand slowing down further. Investment activity has been losing traction. The weakening of the global economy in the face of intensifying trade and geo-political tensions has severely impacted India's exports, which may further impact investment activity, going forward. Private consumption, which has been the mainstay of domestic demand, has also decelerated. The slowing down of domestic demand is also reflected in significant moderation in CPI inflation excluding food and fuel; and contraction in merchandise imports.

In view of weakening of domestic growth impulses and unsettled global macroeconomic environment, there is a need to bolster dwindling domestic demand and support investment activity, even as the impact of past three rate cuts is gradually working its way to the real economy. With headline inflation projected to remain within the target over the next one-year horizon, supporting domestic growth by further reducing interest rates needs to be given the utmost priority. Given the current and evolving inflation and growth scenario at this juncture, it can no longer be a business as usual approach. The economy needs a larger push. I am, therefore, of the view that a reduction in the policy repo rate by conventional 25 bps will be inadequate. On the other hand, a 50 bps rate cut might be excessive and indicate a knee jerk reaction. A policy rate adjustment of 25 bps or multiples thereof may not always be consistent with the evolving macroeconomic situation. Hence, at times it is apposite to calibrate the size of the conventional rate adjustment. Considering these aspects, I vote for reducing the policy repo rate by 35 basis points and for continuing with the accommodative stance of monetary policy. The calibration of the size of the rate cut is expected to reinforce and quicken the impact of (i) the past cumulative rate reduction of 75 basis points; (ii) change in the stance from neutral to accommodative; and (iii) injection of large surplus liquidity in the system.

Source: RBI

Appendix VI (Ref: Multiple Objectives, One Policy)

Excerpts from the Inaugural Address by Shri Shaktikanta Das, Governor, Reserve Bank of India delivered at FIBAC 2019 – the Annual Global Banking Conference organised by Indian Banks' Association (IBA) and Federation of Indian Chambers of Commerce and Industry (FICCI) in Mumbai on Monday, August 19, 2019

Emerging Challenges to Financial Stability

The Indian Scenario

The pursuit of financial stability has always been a policy priority in India. The twin concerns of monetary and financial stability constitute the core objectives of the Reserve Bank. Similar to the global case, India also responded to the crisis by introducing changes in the existing institutional architecture to further the cause of financial stability. Recognising the various channels that could lead to systemic instability and the fact that different segments of financial systems are regulated by different regulators, the institutional mechanisms of the Financial Stability Development Council (FSDC), under the Chairmanship of the Finance Minister, and the FSDC sub-committee, under the chairmanship of Governor, Reserve Bank, have been fully functional. The biannual Financial Stability Report (FSR), a report of FSDC sub-committee, analyses the current state of financial system, the extent of interconnectedness among its various segments and possible sources of vulnerabilities that could impact domestic financial stability.

The headwinds to financial stability could emanate from various sectors of the economy, namely, (i) the credit market; (ii) financial markets; (iii) external sector; and (iv) payment system. It may emanate from some other sources as well. But today, I will focus on these four aspects.

Headwinds from Banking Sector

In India, the credit market is dominated by the banking sector which plays a key role in financial intermediation in the economy. Soundness of the banking system may have a bearing on the financial stability through various channels – excessive credit growth; maturity mismatches and liquidity issues; high proportion of non-performing loans; and overleveraging, among others. Even if individual institutions are robust, the overall behaviour of the financial sector can pose a systemic risk. Hence, monitoring the health of the banking sector is crucial for financial stability.

In recent years, as a result of efforts by both the Reserve Bank and the Government, the overhang of stressed assets in the banking system has declined. Going forward, the macro-stress tests for credit risk conducted by the Reserve Bank indicate that under the baseline scenario, the GNPA ratio may decline further by March 20202. Other indicators like the provision coverage ratio (PCR), capital adequacy and return on assets have also improved. I have earlier stressed that the real test of performance, efficiency, internal stability and governance improvement in public sector banks (PSBs) would be their ability to access capital markets rather than looking at the Government as a recapitaliser of first and last resort.

Financial Stability Report, June 2019, Reserve Bank of India.

Despite certain teething problems, the Insolvency and Bankruptcy Code (IBC) is proving to be a game changer. New norms for resolution of stressed assets framed in June 2019 by the Reserve Bank provide incentives for early resolution, with discretion to lenders on resolution processes. The objective is to ring-fence future build-ups of NPA stress and protect the banking sector. The recent amendments to the IBC should also be able to facilitate faster resolution of stressed assets.

As we have seen in the recent past, the build-up of risks among regulated entities due to interconnectedness, exposure concentrations, non-transparent market practices, governance deficiencies, and their contagion effects have repercussions for financial stability. In this regard, the Reserve Bank is keeping a close watch on the interconnectedness of banks and non-banks. The Working Group on Core Investment Companies (CICs) has already started its deliberations and based on its recommendations, the Reserve Bank proposes to carry out necessary changes in the regulatory architecture for CICs. We are also in the process of building a specialised regulatory and supervisory cadre for regulation and supervision of banks and non-banks.

Another important issue in this context is the immediate need to strengthen corporate governance structure in banks, which I have elaborated earlier as well. This would include efficient functioning of their boards and board sub-committees, especially audit and risk management committees; robust system for monitoring of performance of MDs/CEOs; and, an effective performance evaluation system to improve the financial and operating parameters of banks. We have already sent our suggestions to the Government for governance reforms in PSBs. Overall, it is important that risk management systems, compliance functions, and internal control mechanisms are strengthened and made more dynamic.

Non-Banking Sector

Coming to the NBFC sector, we all know that this sector complements the banking sector and aspires to act as the bridge to provide last mile connectivity. Further, niche NBFCs fulfil the unmet and exclusive credit needs of infrastructure, factoring, leasing and other such activities. Non-traditional and digital players are now entering this space to deliver financial services by way of innovative methods involving digital platform. There is a web of inter-linkages of the NBFC sector with the banking sector, capital market and other financial sector entities. The Reserve Bank keeps a close watch on these inter-linkages to ensure financial stability. With a view to strengthen the sector, maintain stability and avoid regulatory arbitrage, the Reserve Bank and the Government have been proactively taking necessary regulatory and supervisory steps. It is our endeavour to have an optimal level of regulation and supervision so that the NBFC sector is financially resilient and robust. We will not hesitate to take whatever steps are required to maintain financial stability in the short, medium and the long-term.

Our objective is to harmonise the liquidity norms between banks and NBFCs, taking into account their unique business models. We are also looking at governance and risk management structures in NBFCs. Recently in May 2019, NBFCs with a size of more than ₹5,000 crores have been advised to appoint a functionally independent Chief Risk

Officer (CRO) with clearly specified role and responsibilities. This is expected to bring in professional risk management to the working of large NBFCs.

The move to bring Housing Finance Companies (HFCs) under the regulatory ambit of the Reserve Bank is significant, given their asset-liability profiles. Including HFCs, the size of the NBFC sector constitutes about 25 per cent of combined balance sheet of scheduled commercial banks. The Reserve Bank will take necessary measures to deal with these challenges.

Source: RBI

RBI's Functional Freedom

Two articles, one by former Chairman of SEBI and Life Insurance Corporation of India C G N Bajpai (January 22, 2019, The many nuances of regulatory autonomy) and another by Subir Roy (January 24, 2019, "How do great institutions come into being?") published in Business Standard in quick succession give an opportunity for a healthy debate on the background in which controversy is persisting about the contours of functional freedom enjoyed by statutory bodies and government-owned Public Sector Undertakings. Here we will briefly discuss what was behind the alleged government-RBI spar which resulted in the resignation of RBI Governor on December 10, 2018 and the possible reasons for appointment of a former bureaucrat as his replacement.

The basic issues behind the government-RBI spar need to be addressed by the political leadership in public interest as they are cancerous and may affect the functional freedom of all organizations which handle money. Simply put, they arise from Finance Ministry's inept handling of fiscal deficit. To cover up its own imprudent management of nation's monetary resources, it has become habitual for the Finance Ministry to use the government's 'ownership rights' over statutory bodies and PSUs to force funds diversion to the Consolidated Fund of India. The methods included (a) asking institutions like LIC to retain liquid funds to be available at call for diversion, (b) forcing PSUs and statutory bodies to inflate surplus income and declare dividends. A stage has come when 'advance against future dividends' is demanded from organizations like RBI.

It is time, an expert committee comprising professionals with expertise in international accounting practices as members supported by representatives of GOI, CAG and RBI studies the money-management by the central finance ministry.

The suggestion is in the context of the casual approach to fiscal policy evidenced in the recent past. Illustratively:

a. Finance Ministry has been looking at PSUs as fund-raising organizations. Ministry exerts pressure on PSUs to declare dividend, ignoring institutional priorities on income and surpluses.

b. GOI expects institutions like LIC to maintain surplus liquid funds on an ongoing basis, to be available for diversion at short notice.

c. Last year, RBI was persuaded to make advance transfer of funds to GOI against year-end (RBI's financial year is July-June) transfer of surplus income. RBI Act doesn't envisage such payments. Dr. Rajan had mentioned this in his September 3, 2016 Delhi speech (That is not an issue though, as GOI can always introduce new provisions.)

The real solution to the problem of persisting gap between revenue receipts and rising development expenditure lies in mapping nation's wealth remaining unaccounted and considering a realistic taxation policy which should cover high income groups and agricultural income. But, such a diagnosis and prescription of remedial measures won't be acceptable to the media or political leadership. Let us go deeper.

Media interpretations of the differences in policy perceptions between the government and the RBI had created an impression that the three predecessors of the present RBI Governor Shaktikanta Das were fighting for independence from the government, whereas all they talked about was functional autonomy in policy formulation and implementation within the contours of statute book. No RBI governor had ever threatened the government of operating monetary policy parallel to the fiscal policy.

RBI's Accountability

Former RBI Governor Bimal Jalan, who chaired the Economic Capital Framework Panel appointed by the Reserve Bank of India (RBI) reportedly said in an interview given to *Reuters* during the second week of January 2019 that "The RBI is accountable to the government for executing the kind of monetary policy that has been announced." What the former governor chose to say then, left people guessing, as Jalan had said the obvious.

After the Monetary Policy Committee (MPC) came into being, RBI announces the monetary policy based on the majority view taken by the MPC after due deliberations at its meetings spread over 3 days once in every two months. MPC which has statutory backing has three members including Governor from RBI and three experts nominated by GOI. In such committees, once constituted, members apply their independent minds in deliberations and decisions are taken in public interest. A practice different from legislatures where political parties can use a whip. Governor who chairs MPC has a casting vote, not to give RBI any specific advantage, but keeping in view the chances for a tie because of the even number (6) membership. In a way, all members of MPC are GOI nominees as Governor and his deputies are appointed by GOI. In the circumstances how the thought of RBI going back on monetary policy announced by it came to Dr. Jalan's mind is intriguing.

All along, RBI and government at the highest level had interaction on major policy issues and where a difference in view cropped up government's views prevailed. This is normal as government of the day will always have, and should have, the upper hand, as after all, government has the responsibility and power to legislate. Viewed from this angle, the whole speculations about GOI invoking Section 7 of the RBI Act which preceded Urjit Patel's resignation on December 10, 2018 were based on misinformation.

RBI's Subservience to GOI

Reserve Bank of India, by design, is not meant to be subservient to Government of India. Those who drafted the Reserve Bank of India Act during the second quarter of last century were well aware of the conflict of interest between Fiscal and Monetary policies. Those who are watching the current media debate on relationship issues between GOI and RBI need to read again the Sections 7, 8 (see Appendix VII) and 58 of the Reserve Bank of India Act, 1934 which are about the management of RBI. There is no ambiguity in the provisions about the government's control over the management of RBI. The provisions of Section 7 of the RBI Act relating to issue of directions to RBI by GOI will be useful only for RBI governor to get himself armed to make a recalcitrant board which tries to overlook GOI's policies, while taking decisions, see reason.

Appendix VII (Ref: RBI's Functional Freedom)

RBI Act provisions on management of RBI

Reserve Bank of India Act, 1934

Section 7

Management

The Central Government may from time to time give such directions to the Bank as it may, after consultation with the Governor of the Bank, consider necessary in the public interests.

Subject to any such directions, the general superintendence and direction of the affairs and business of the Bank shall be entrusted to a Central Board of Directors which may exercise all powers and do all acts and things which may be exercised or done by the Bank.

Save as otherwise provided in regulations made by the Central Board, the Governor and in his absence the Deputy Governor nominated by him in his behalf, shall also have powers of general superintendence and direction of the affairs and the business of the Bank, and may exercise all powers and do all acts and things which may be exercised or done by the Bank.

Section 8

Composition of the Central Board, and term of office of directors

The Central Board shall consist of the following Directors, namely:-

a. a Governor and not more than four Deputy Governors to be appointed by the Central Government;

b. four Directors to be nominated by the Central Government, one from each of the four Local Boards as constituted by section 9;

c. ten Directors to be nominated by the Central Government; and

d. one Government official to be nominated by the Central Government.

The Governor and Deputy Governors shall devote their whole time to the affairs of the Bank, and shall receive such salaries and allowances as may be determined by the Central Board, with the approval of the Central Government:

PROVIDED that the Central Board may, if in its opinion it is necessary in the public interest so to do, permit the Governor or a Deputy Governor to undertake, at the request of the Central Government or any State Government, such part-time honorary work, whether related to the purposes of this Act or not, as is not likely to interfere with his duties as Governor or Deputy Governor, as the case may be:

[PROVIDED FURTHER that the Central Government may, in consultation with the Bank, appoint a Deputy Governor as the Chairman of the National Bank, on such terms and conditions as that Government may specify.]

A Deputy Governor and the Director nominated under clause (d) of sub-section (1) may attend any meeting of the Central Board and take part in its deliberations but shall not be entitled to vote:

PROVIDED that when the Governor is, for any reason, unable to attend any such meeting, a Deputy Governor authorized by him in this behalf in writing may vote for him at that meeting.

The Governor and a Deputy Governor shall hold office for such term not exceeding five years as the Central Government may fix when appointing them, and shall be eligible for re-appointment.

A Director nominated under clause (c) of sub-section (1) shall hold office for a period of four years and thereafter until his successor shall have been nominated.

A Director nominated under clause (d) of sub-section (1) shall hold office during the pleasure of the Central Government.

No act or proceeding of the Board shall be questioned on the ground merely of the existence of any vacancy in, or any defect in the constitution, of the board.

A retiring director shall be eligible for re-nomination.

End Note: Sections 7, 8 and 58 of the RBI Act, 1934 broadly define the contours of RBI management.

Source: RBI

Reserve Bank of India: What Lies Ahead?

"Having met with staunch criticisms for mass mismanagement of public money in the wake of the 2019 elections, the current government is valiantly trying to save its face. Invoking Section 7 is a saving grace for several reasons. It can earn the government a clean chit by validating its blaming of the RBI, and in so doing can build up political pressure on the central bank to dilute its regulatory policies in order to favour political clientele, and even stretch such pressure to siphon off the bank's (internal) reserves over and above the surpluses transferable to the government, all for supporting its populist rhetoric."

—Excerpts from Editorial, Economic & Political Weekly, November 3, 2018

The quote above sums up the media perception of the developments that led to the resignation of Urjit Patel as RBI Governor on December 10, 2018. I am not sure whether anyone who has been commenting on the developments in the Indian Economy will be able to make a balanced analysis of the current confusion in people's mind about the GOI-RBI relationship. As we have no constituency interests to protect, let us make a beginning.

Those who drafted the Reserve Bank of India Act during the second quarter of last century were well aware of the conflict of interest between Fiscal and Monetary policies. Those who are watching the current media debate on relationship issues between GOI and RBI need to read again the Sections 7, 8 (see Appendix IX) and 58 of the Reserve Bank of India Act, 1934 which are about the management of RBI.

A media report captioned "RBI, govt spar over panel head" published in a financial newspaper in the first half of November 2018 covered the glaring disagreements between RBI and GOI on some of the issues which led media to speculate about the imminent exit of the then RBI Governor Urjit Patel and one/some of his deputies.

In reality, GOI and RBI had come out with two equally competent economists, namely Dr. Bimal Jalan (GOI nominee) and Dr. Rakesh Mohan (RBI nominee) to chair the panel to review India's central bank's economic capital framework (ECF). My response was, prudence demanded inclusion of both the celebrity economists with Indian background in the ECF Panel, as their rich experience in RBI and GOI besides their association with global financial/research organizations would enable the panel to have informed deliberations. The possibility of Dr. Jalan, considering his own political leanings, himself moving out in favour of allowing his former colleague Dr. Rakesh Mohan to head the Panel was also not ruled out. Media suggestion was to allow both to co-chair the panel, which was also not a bad idea. I felt that both were mature and seasoned statesmen and would know how to conduct the deliberations keeping the national interest uppermost. In the circumstances, I exclude the possibility of this issue having triggered the abrupt exit of Urjit Patel.

RBI's capital, since inception remains static at Rs. 50 million. Bank's reserves (Contingency Fund + Asset Development Fund) depleted from a self-set target of 12 percent of total assets (which RBI almost touched in 2009) to a low of 7.05 percent of total assets as on June 30, 2018. The percentage was 9.2 in 2014 from which year RBI continuously transferred its entire surplus income to GOI till 2016 resulting in depletion of this percentage every year since then, as the central bank balance sheet grew in size. Earlier GOI listens to the alarm, the better for the Indian economy. Ideally, the ECF Panel should have first arrived at a decent figure to be recommended as RBI's share capital (say, upwards of the equivalent of US $ 200 billion, which itself will be too low, considering the responsibilities of India's central bank). Needless to emphasize, RBI would also need a reasonably higher level of 'liquid' reserves. Keeping all these in view, the ECF Panel could have considered creation of a "Capital Protection Fund" (in addition to the reserves) to be augmented by annual contributions from Bank's income.

The personal note posted by Dr. Urjit Patel at RBI's website on December 10, 2018 is in Appendix VIII. Reports show that his resignation was accepted by GOI next day and new Governor Shaktikanta Das took charge on December 12, 2018.

I would like to substitute 'responding to call of conscience' for 'personal reasons' in the brief statement issued by Urjit Patel immediately after stepping down as RBI Governor. And, the substituted words include 'personal reasons' some of which do not remain secret anymore. But, for those personal reasons, Patel would not have left the institution in the lurch. Real reasons are national and not personal. For some clue, let us recall another incident, taking you back in India's history to 1975.

Sankara Pillai had run Shanker's Weekly for decades, almost single-handed. He closed down the Weekly with a 'Souvenir,' last issue of the Weekly appearing in July 1975, that is within almost a month from the declaration of National Emergency. Shanker could have 'compromised' and continued to publish the Weekly. He said, 'Weekly could have taken the Emergency in its stride.' He closed it down for 'personal reasons.' And those reasons included avoiding embarrassment and uncertainties to certain individuals and families who were part of the Weekly.

Each individual is different. GOI's choices to man the top positions in RBI, beginning with Dr. Raghuram Rajan as Governor have been non-controversial and excellent, viewed from the angle of professional competence. It would be interesting to think how Dr. Bimal Jalan or Dr. Y V Reddy or Dr. Rajan would have responded to the situation Urjit Patel faced in the third year of his governorship. Also, it is worth pondering over as to whether things would have been different if the position of RBI Governor was more secure. These thoughts I will leave here with a quote from my own article on the appointment of Dr. Raghuram Rajan as Governor, RBI published in the September 2013 issue of The Global ANALYST. I said:

"…The only negative in the whole affair is, as on several occasions in the past, once again GOI has opted for a short-term appointment. This time it should have been for a five-year term in the first instance itself. We are not privy to the information as to whether the decision to appoint Rajan for 3 years was because of a casual/cut & paste' from previous appointment orders or because GOI thought, if friction between RBI and GOI persists, changing RBI Governor is a soft option. As someone in the media has already observed, the flipside is, if things do not go well, Dr. Rajan could choose an assignment anywhere, a choice, many in top positions in India do not have. Ideally, RBI Governor should have a tenure of 5 to 10 years…"

Thanks to the support the institution received from GOI from the very inception till today, Reserve Bank of India never had to succumb to injuries like this. The signals from the press release issued by RBI after the Central Board meeting on December 14, 2018 and the media responses given by the new Governor Shaktikanta Das before and after the first board meeting he presided over, were positive. He too started talking RBI's language, once he arrived at Mint Road, much faster than his IAS-predecessors.

Appendix VIII (Ref: Reserve Bank of India: What Lies Ahead?)

RBI accepts the challenge

I

Statement by Governor

On account of personal reasons, I have decided to step down from my current position effective immediately. It has been my privilege and honour to serve in the Reserve Bank of India in various capacities over the years. The support and hard work of RBI staff, officers and management has been the proximate driver of the Bank's considerable accomplishments in recent years. I take this opportunity to express gratitude to my colleagues and Directors of the RBI Central Board, and wish them all the best for the future.

Urjit R. Patel

10th December 2018

II

RBI Press Release: 2018–2019/1362

December 12, 2018

Shri Shaktikanta Das appointed as Governor of RBI

Shri Shaktikanta Das, IAS Retd., former Secretary, Department of Revenue and Department of Economic Affairs, Ministry of Finance, Government of India assumed charge as the 25th Governor of the Reserve Bank of India effective December 12, 2018. Immediately prior to his current assignment, he was acting as Member, 15th Finance Commission and G20 Sherpa of India. Shri Shaktikanta Das has vast experience in various areas of governance in the last 38 years. Shri Das has held important positions in the Central and State Governments in the areas of Finance, Taxation, Industries, Infrastructure, etc. During his long tenure in the Ministry of Finance, Government of India, he was directly associated with the preparation of as many as 8 Union

Budgets. Shri Das has also served as India's Alternate Governor in the World Bank, Asian Development Bank (ADB), New Development Bank (NDB) and Asian Infrastructure Investment Bank (AIIB). He has represented India in international fora like the IMF, G20, BRICS, SAARC, etc. Shri Shaktikanta Das is a postgraduate from St. Stephen's College, Delhi University.

Jose J. Kattoor

Chief General Manager

III

RBI Central Board meets in Mumbai

The Reserve Bank of India's (RBI) Central Board met today in Mumbai under the Chairmanship of Shri Shaktikanta Das, Governor, Reserve Bank of India. The Central Board placed on record its appreciation of the valuable services rendered by Dr. Urjit R. Patel during his tenure as Governor and Deputy Governor of the Bank. The Board deliberated on the Governance Framework of the Reserve Bank and it was decided that the matter required further examination. The Board reviewed, inter alia, the current economic situation, global and domestic challenges, matters relating to liquidity and credit delivery to the economy, and issues related to currency management and financial literacy. The draft report on Trend and Progress of Banking in India (2017–18) was also discussed.

Jose J. Kattoor

Chief General Manager

Press Release: 2018–2019/1375

Source: RBI Website

India's Central Bank: Challenges Galore I

The idea of an independent central bank was conceived in the 1920's and the Reserve Bank of India came into being on April 1, 1935, after enactment of the Reserve Bank of India Act, 1934.

Even while giving shape to a reasonably strong central bank for India in the situations prevailing during the early 1930's, the need for comprehensive changes in the Reserve Bank of India Act, 1934 at a later date had been foreseen by the writers of the Act who included the following clauses in the Preamble of the RBI Act:

"And Whereas in the present disorganization of the monetary systems of the world it is not possible to determine what is suitable as a permanent basis for the Indian monetary system;

But Whereas it is expedient to make temporary provision on the basis of the existing monetary system, and to leave the question of the monetary standard best suited to India to be considered when the international monetary position has become sufficiently clear and stable to make it possible to frame permanent measures;"

But, even the authors of the original RBI Act would not have anticipated the kind of assault on RBI that is happening during the current decade, with tacit approval from the owners.

The unfolding story of the humiliation India's central bank is being subjected to, and which, so far, has been taken in its stride by RBI, has been brilliantly narrated by Dr. Rakesh Mohan in a three-part series on

RBI, published in the Business Standard recently (October 3–5, 2018). Expressing anguish about the destabilization efforts by vested interests faced by RBI, he concludes that the amendment to the Preamble of the Reserve Bank of India Act, 1934 carried out in 2016 was intended to implement various recommendations of Committees like Percy Mistry Committee (2007), Raghuram Rajan Committee (2009), and Financial Sector Legislative Reforms Committee (2013, Chairman: B N Srikrishna). In effect, deviating from the purported mandate of considering Financial Sector Reforms FSLRC made several recommendations, if implemented, would have truncated and destabilized RBI in one stroke. Though some acts and omissions on the part of Raghuram Rajan during his three-year tenure at Mint Road were controversial, his short-duration presence in India helped in diluting the adverse impact of FSLRC on RBI and two consecutive Economic Surveys on the National Balance Sheet. Once he understood the negatives, Rajan used his teaching skills to make the powers that be understand his point of view, when necessary, by making a PowerPoint presentation himself.

The amended Preamble of the RBI Act now reads as under:

"PREAMBLE

An Act to constitute a Reserve Bank of India.

Whereas it is expedient to constitute a Reserve Bank for India to regulate the issue of Bank notes and the keeping of reserves with a view to securing monetary stability in 2 [India] and generally to operate the currency and credit system of the country to its advantage; 3 [AND WHEREAS it is essential to have a modern monetary policy framework to meet the challenge of an increasingly complex economy; AND WHEREAS the primary objective of the monetary policy is to maintain price stability while keeping in mind the objective of growth; AND WHEREAS the monetary policy framework in India shall be operated by the Reserve Bank of India;] It is hereby enacted as follows:-"

Dr. Rakesh Mohan's observation that "The RBI has been a full-service central bank since its inception in 1935, encompassing its role, inter alia, as a monetary authority, a banking regulator, the lender of last resort, a foreign exchange and exchange rate manager, and a sovereign debt manager, apart from other functions such as currency issuer and payment system regulator and facilitator." need to receive the serious attention it deserves from the policymakers. RBI has also played its role excellently well at appropriate times in reorganizing the institutional system in the financial sector to meet the country's economic development needs. Establishment of SBI, IDBI, NABARD, Exim Bank, SIDBI, and RRBs, timely interventions to avoid bank failures and the developmental role played by it to ensure successful implementation of government programmes aimed at alleviation of poverty and providing infrastructure for economic development are initiatives from RBI for which there may not be any parallel in the history of central banks.

All these and more leads to the question as to why efforts are being made to weaken RBI. Beyond direct threats of weakening the central bank by legislative procedure, there are constant efforts at making RBI subservient to certain vested interests. These are in the form of weakening RBI's board (On November 8, 2016, the day of demonetization, out of 14 positions on the RBI Central board, 8 were vacant, according to a source) and top management. By design, all Governors and most of the Deputy Governors, of late, are getting a tenure of 3 years and the position at Executive Directors' level is also not much better. Ideally, the tenure at these levels should be 5 years and above.

Regulation and Supervision

Chapter VI of RBI Annual Report 2017–18 (See Appendix IX) dwells in detail about the work in progress in the areas of Regulation, Supervision, and Financial Stability. In addition to commercial banks in public and private sectors, there are a host of other institutions in Indian Financial Sector many of which carry on banking and 'quasi-banking' functions which are also gradually being brought under the regulatory discipline of RBI. These include cooperatives including cooperative banks and NBFCs (some of which are government-owned). The multiplicity of ownership and applicability of several laws in addition to the Banking Regulation Act and RBI Act pose a variety of practical problems for RBI in enforcing prudential business norms and regulatory discipline over such institutions.

Add to all these the constraints, like the not very supportive approach from the owner (GOI) faced by RBI expressed through the constant threats of dilution of powers and the demand for transfer of more funds resulting in depletion of RBI's reserves and so on.

Some HR Issues

In Chapter I (Assessment and Prospects) of the Annual Report, 2018–19, RBI has observed:

"The stage is set for the intensification of structural reforms that will unlock new growth energies and place the Indian economy on a sustainable trajectory of higher growth. Resolute progress in repairing and resolving the acute stress in the banking system and in shoring up corporate debt will re-intermediate financial flows for productive purposes, which are essential for sustaining an acceleration in growth with macroeconomic and financial stability."

For preparing the ground for this and constant monitoring of compliance with regulatory requirements by banks and other institutions RBI needs to strengthen its workforce numerically and from the angle of skill-development factoring in the needs of expanding work areas. RBI's position is similar to Fire Force and Air Force, as regards maintenance and upkeep of manpower and 'tools' ready to act any time. Complacency can be suicidal and outsourcing work is no option. These observations are in the context of RBI's staff strength remaining static (around 7000 officers and 4000 clerks) during the two years 2016 and 2017 when workload had increased considerably, compared to, say that existed at the beginning of the decade.

Protecting the RBI's Balance Sheet

Dr. Rakesh Mohan in the concluding part of the three-part series of articles published in the Business Standard which I recalled at the beginning, has used stronger language to defend the need to protect RBI's Balance Sheet. He said:

"The most disturbing developments in recent years have been formal suggestions emanating from the government's official statutory

Economic Survey proposing a raid on the RBI's balance sheet, with the purpose of funding the recapitalization of public sector banks. The proposal was to transfer a portion of the stock of securities held in the RBI's balance sheet to public sector banks. It was argued that the RBI has excess capital in its balance sheet."

Dr. Rakesh Mohan has argued the case for a strong RBI balance sheet basing his arguments on the functional responsibilities like monetary policy operations, shouldered by RBI which can't wait for budget funding. Here we remember S S Tarapore who retired as RBI Deputy Governor and continued as a strong defender of the central bank's interests till his death, with respect and gratitude. Asserting that fears with regard to possible central bank losses are not illusory, he mentioned that according to the BIS 43 out of 108 central banks reported losses for at least one year between 1984 and 2005. One can imagine a political response, like "So what? The owner (GOI) can always make good the losses!"

The answer to that is, the financial stability of the country is important to attract investments from within the country and abroad and a weak central bank doesn't send out positive signals in this regard.

In a carefully worded statement, RBI Annual Report, 2017–18 took cognizance of the need to augment capital and reserves to a reasonably high level in Chapter XI (see Appendix X). RBI's capital since inception remains static at Rs. 5 crore. Bank's reserves (Contingency Fund + Asset Development Fund) depleted from a self-set target of 12 percent of total assets (which RBI almost touched in 2009) to a low of 7.05 percent of total assets as on June 30, 2018. The percentage was 9.2 in 2014 from which year RBI continuously transferred its entire surplus income to GOI till 2016 resulting in depletion of this percentage every year since then. Earlier GOI listens to the alarm, the better for the Indian economy.

Appendix IX (Ref: India's Central Bank: Challenges Galore I)

RBI Annual Report 2018

Excerpts from Chapter VI Regulation, Supervision and Financial Stability

Introductory

During 2017–18, the banking sector continued to grapple with the problems of deteriorating asset quality and declining profitability. In order to align the resolution process with the Insolvency and Bankruptcy Code (IBC), 2016, the framework for the resolution of stressed assets was revised and the previous schemes were withdrawn. Customer rights were strengthened by limiting liability of customers in unauthorized electronic banking transactions. Further, given the increasing popularity of digital payments medium, data protection and cyber security norms were strengthened. For effective and timely redressal of grievances of customers of Non-Banking Financial Companies (NBFCs), an Ombudsman Scheme for deposit taking NBFCs was initiated. Regulatory policies for cooperative banks were further harmonized with those of scheduled commercial banks (SCBs). In order to bring about ownership-neutral regulations, government-owned NBFCs will be required to adhere to the Bank's prudential regulations in a phased manner.

Appendix X (Ref: India's Central Bank: Challenges Galore I)

Box XI.1(RBI Annual Report 2017–18)

Surplus Distribution Policy in Central Banks:

An Overview

It is in the public interest that a central bank should continue to perform its public policy functions effectively even during times of extreme stress. A central bank, therefore, requires a minimum level of confidence regarding its financial strength and the resources at its disposal which will allow it to effectively discharge its functions even during crises. The surplus distribution policy adopted by a central bank is one of the key elements that can determine its financial strength.

Major factors determining surplus distribution

The same approach for surplus distribution cannot be applied across central banks considering the varied political and economic environment under which they operate. Other considerations which necessitate different distribution policies are the varying levels of risk exposures of the central banks as well as the availability of risk transfer mechanisms between the central banks and their stakeholders. The risk transfer mechanism may also not be effective if a particular stakeholder's finances are also under stress during a crisis.

Various approaches adopted for surplus transfer

A cross country analysis of the surplus distribution policy of central banks by scrutinising publicly available information reveals that central banks can be classified predominantly into the following categories of surplus distribution:

a. Surplus retention is based on a target level of provisions to be achieved. A few central banks also follow accelerated surplus retention based on a target level of provisions in case where the target is not met.

b. Retention of surplus is based on a numerical rule linked to the surplus of the current year.

c. Surplus smoothening wherein it is ensured that regular surplus may be transferred to the government and that the surplus transfer is not affected by the cyclicality of the provisions of the central bank.

Desirable characteristics of a Surplus Distribution Policy

The provisioning requirements of a central bank should be linked to a target level of financial resilience to be achieved/maintained. In the case of central banks where the distribution arrangements result in continuous substantial transfers without considering the overall level of provisions and risk transfer mechanisms, the financial strength of the central bank may progressively weaken. Further, if a central bank maintains unrealised valuation gains on its balance sheet, these are predominantly taken as non-distributable.

The distribution policy should also bring about smoothening of surplus transfer to the government.

India's Central Bank: Challenges Galore II

"Repeated government allusions to a $5 trillion economy by 2024, which would necessitate steady real growth of at least 8–9 percent per year starting from now, seem increasingly unrealistic."

-Dr. Raghuram Rajan, former RBI Governor in India Today, December 16, 2019

We need to take cognizance of the timing and selective nature of release of information by economists to develop the stories they subsequently build up. Dr. Rajan, perhaps for the first time, has also spoken at different forums about the legacy inherited by the Prime Minister Narendra Modi's government in 2014 from UPA II. He had this to say, in his article published in India Today:

"A large number of infrastructure projects had stalled because of difficulties in land acquisition, lack of inputs like coal or gas, or the slow pace of obtaining government clearances. Existing power producers were running into difficulties as heavily indebted power distribution companies delayed payments or stopped buying. India experienced the absurdity of surplus power capacity even as power demand went unmet. As more promoters ran into financial distress, bad loans on bank balance sheets increased, slowing the flow of new credit.

The agricultural sector was also in a mess. In part, this resulted from decades of misguided government intervention such as distorted pricing and subsidies—which resulted in anomalies such as a water-short nation exporting water-thirsty rice. In part, this resulted from neglect; successive governments did little to eliminate the hordes of middlemen who took their cut as food travelled from the farm to the fork; instead, governments spent scarce resources on loan waivers, a form of misdirected cash transfer, rather than on improving farmer access to new technologies, seeds or land. Prime Minister Modi was elected, not just because his record in Gujarat suggested he would resolve these legacy issues, but also because he promised reforms that would enhance growth and employment."

Just as fiscal policy measures impact central bank's monetary policy, the legacy issues flagged by Dr. Rajan had a lot to do with the chaotic situation in which the Indian Financial Sector in general, and the Public Sector Banks (PSBs) in particular landed in recent times. We must thank the former RBI governor for taking interest in the progress of reform measures he initiated during his stay in India and sharing his views which have the backing of his experience gained in India and abroad on policy formulation and implementation.

As RBI governor Dr. Raghuram Rajan had mentioned the following as principal reasons for rising NPAs while deposing before the Public Accounts Committee:

- Domestic and global slowdown.
- Delays in statutory and other approvals' especially for projects under implementation.
- Aggressive lending practices during upturn, as evidenced from high corporate leverage.
- Laxity in credit risk appraisal and loan monitoring in banks.
- Lack of appraisal of skills for projects that need specialized skills, resulting in acceptance of inflated cost and aggressive projections.
- Willful default, loan fraud and corruption.

Have we Forgotten Traditional Principles of Banking?

Kautilya in Arthashastra incorporated risk and uncertainty to the levels of profit and interest. He had indicated that the higher level of risk and uncertainty must be rewarded by higher profits and interests. He prescribed the allowable profits on imports to be twice of that on domestic goods. Allowable profits on imports was 10 percent whereas it was 5 percent on domestic products. The reason behind this was clear. In those days, the importers of foreign goods had to face great danger of being robbed and looted at the time of shipment of the products from other states. Kautilya's concept of profit is quite similar to the modern days profit theory which states that profit is the reward of uncertainty. Kautilya favored charging interests on loans but the rate of interest was regulated by the state. According to him, rate of interest should be determined by two factors – risk involved and productivity of the capital. The rate of interest was higher for the traders however, it was lower for the personal purpose, such as, marriage or funeral etc. purposes. Furthermore, interest rate was different for different types of trades depending on the riskiness of the venture. Hence it is observed that determination of interest rate considered both elements – risk and productivity of the loan. Human consideration of interest payment was also observed. Certain groups of people, such as, inability to pay, students etc. were exempted from paying interest. However, they had to come through proper legal system to avail such exemption. Hence, differentiated interest rate structure depending on the purpose of loan were prevailed at that time which is very much similar to modern days borrowing and lending system of banks and financial institutions (Source: Kautilya's Arthashastra, Sarkar, 2000).

Though the numbers may undergo change, the principles of banking and economics enunciated by Kautilya in Arthashastra hold good even today. We need to revisit the rationale and evolution of banking in India, perhaps over centuries and in more detail the relevance of money lenders during the last century to set right the house of banking in order.

Till deregulation of interest rates, there was some method in madness, in the factoring-in of the principles of cross-subsidization in prescription of interest rates. Post-deregulation, while interest rates on deposits went by the principle of 'demand and supply,' there was inadequate application of mind in deciding interest rates on loans. Those who borrowed heavily, in thousands of crores, influenced, to an extent interest rates policy also and some banks failed to charge higher interests or prescribe conditionalities making mid-term reviews a professional tool to monitor end-use of loans.

Social control and the nationalization of bigger banks that followed gave an impression that banks are another arm of government to implement welfare measures. Professionalism took a back seat.

Institutions in the Financial Sector

We need to have a relook at the institutional system in the financial sector in India. We have, elsewhere in this book, discussed the problems faced by commercial banks including public sector banks. Here, let us initiate some discussion about cooperative banks and "Non-Banks" which are also facing stressful situation.

Cooperative Banks

The approach to regulating the banking business of cooperatives has been half-hearted ever since 1966 when certain provisions of the Banking Regulation Act 1949 were made applicable to cooperative societies by incorporation of Section 56 in the B R Act.

More than five decades have passed without any serious effort to diagnose and treat the inherent inadequacies in the administrative and supervisory/regulatory architecture that sustains the cooperatives in India. The laxity on the part of legislators in regulating cooperatives professionally is attributable to the vested interests of political parties and local landlords in managing the multiple activities of village level to high profile national level cooperatives.

Since the beginning of last century when cooperative movement emerged on the Indian scene, cooperatives have been playing a proactive role in the economic development and social life in this country. Attempts by vested interests to capture and manage cooperative institutions and resultant efforts to circumvent regulatory and supervisory requirements did affect the growth of this ideal institutional system, off and on, since certain provisions of the Banking Regulation Act, 1949 were made applicable to cooperative societies. The problems faced by cooperative banks during demonetization (2016), the present state of affairs at the Mumbai-based multi-state PMC Bank and the genesis of the ambitious proposal to set up Kerala Bank can be traced to inadequacies in managing cooperatives.

The present initiatives to overhaul cooperatives should, inter alia, keep in view the following:

- Need to separate banking business from other activities undertaken by cooperatives and ear-marking administrative, regulatory and supervisory responsibilities to appropriate agencies. This is necessary as both central and state governments are involved in the administration of cooperatives.
- To retain the cooperative character with members' participation, examine whether Multi-state urban cooperative banks should be made federations of state level units.
- Consider whether it would be advantageous to convert urban cooperative banks, like the proposed Kerala Bank which want to expand business and go commercial and do universal banking as banking companies.

The present challenges add to GOI's and RBI's responsibility to ensure that the dual control (state government having a major role in management matters and RBI's regulatory and supervisory role) does not adversely affect the cooperative institutions' smooth functioning.

Some legislative and administrative changes are being thought of, following the PMC Bank failure.

"Non-Banks"

For most of the ills in the financial sector, of late, it has become fashionable to blame the Reserve Bank of India (RBI). The role of "Non-Banks" affecting the smooth functioning of the financial system is much more today than, say, a decade before. The IL&FS and DHFL debt default imbroglio and even the failure of Punjab and Maharashtra Cooperative (PMC) Bank can be traced to exploitation of banking system through back-door by "Non-Banks." This issue is being addressed by RBI by prescribing a liquidity-risk management framework for NBFCs and core investment companies (CICs). Simultaneously, RBI has relaxed end-use stipulation under external commercial borrowing framework for corporates and NBFCs.

RBI's Role

Everyone knows inflation-fighting is not and should not be the principal business of Reserve Bank of India. But certain developments during the decade that is coming to an end gave such an impression in the public mind. This feeling was reaffirmed by the legalization of Monetary Policy Committee (MPC) with a given mandate of keeping inflation at 4 plus or minus 2 percent. One cannot blame RBI for its December 2019 MPC decision not to touch base rates, as the inflation was moving nearer to the upper limit of 6 percent. RBI was also aware that, after cutting the policy repo rate by a cumulative 135 basis points in the previous five bi-monthly policy reviews beginning February 2019, the rate transmission down the layers was not to the level expected and it was prudent to pause and watch.

It is comforting to see that RBI has woken up to the task of infusing order into the institutional system in the financial sector. The statement on Developmental and Regulatory Policies issued along with the Monetary Policy Statement in December 2019 gives sufficient indications to this effect (See excerpts in Appendix XI). Certainly, the bank has its task cut out: fix it, it's broken.

Appendix XI (Ref: India's Central Bank: Challenges Galore II)

Primary (Urban) Co-operative Banks – Exposure Limits and Priority Sector Lending

(RBI Announcement on December 6, 2019)

With a view to reducing concentration risk in the exposures of primary (urban) co-operative banks (UCBs) and to further strengthen the role of UCBs in promoting financial inclusion, it is proposed to amend certain regulatory guidelines relating to UCBs. The guidelines would primarily relate to exposure norms for single and group/interconnected borrowers, promotion of financial inclusion, priority sector lending, etc. These measures are expected to strengthen the resilience and sustainability of UCBs and protect the interest of depositors. An appropriate timeframe will be provided for compliance with the revised norms. A draft circular proposing the above changes for eliciting stakeholder comments will be issued shortly.

Primary (Urban) Co-operative Banks – Reporting to Central Repository of Information on Large Credits (CRILC)

The Reserve Bank has created a Central Repository of Information on Large Credits (CRILC) of scheduled commercial banks, all India financial institutions and certain non-banking financial companies with multiple objectives, which, among others, include strengthening offsite supervision and early recognition of financial distress. With a view to building a similar database of large credits extended by primary (urban) co-operative banks (UCBs), it has been decided to bring UCBs with assets of ₹500 crores and above under the CRILC reporting framework.

Comprehensive Cyber Security Framework for Primary (Urban) Cooperative Banks (UCBs) – A Graded Approach

The Reserve Bank had prescribed a set of baseline cyber security controls for primary (Urban) cooperative banks (UCBs) in October 2018. On further examination, it has been decided to prescribe a comprehensive cyber security framework for the UCBs, as a graded approach, based on their digital depth and interconnectedness with the payment systems landscape, digital products offered by them and assessment of cyber security risk. The framework would mandate implementation of progressively stronger security measures based on the nature, variety and scale of digital product offerings of banks. Such measures would, among others, include implementation of bank specific email domain; periodic security assessment of public facing websites/applications; strengthening the cybersecurity incident reporting mechanism; strengthening of governance framework; and setting up of Security Operations Center (SOC). This would bolster cyber security preparedness and ensure that the UCBs offering a range of payment services and higher Information Technology penetration are brought at par with commercial banks in addressing cyber security threats..

NBFCs – Peer to Peer Lending Platform (NBFC-P2P)

The Reserve Bank had issued directions for Non-Banking Financial Company-Peer to Peer Lending platform (NBFC-P2P) on October 4, 2017. At present, the aggregate limits for both borrowers and lenders across all P2P platforms stand at ₹10 lakh, whereas exposure of a single lender to a single borrower is capped at ₹50,000 across all NBFC-P2P platforms. A review of the functioning of the lending platforms and lending limit was carried out and it has been decided that in order to give the next push to the lending platforms, the aggregate exposure of a lender to all borrowers at any point of time, across all P2P platforms, shall be subject to a cap of ₹50 lakh. Further, it is also proposed to do away with the current requirement of escrow accounts to be operated by bank promoted trustee for transfer of funds having to be necessarily opened with the concerned bank. This will help provide more flexibility in operations. Necessary instructions in this regard will be issued shortly.

Baseline Cyber Security Controls for ATM Switch application service providers of RBI regulated entities

A number of commercial banks, urban cooperative banks and other regulated entities are dependent upon third party application service providers for shared services for ATM Switch applications. Since these service providers also have exposure to the payment system landscape and are, therefore, exposed to the associated cyber threats, it has been decided that certain baseline cyber security controls shall be mandated by the regulated entities in their contractual agreements with these service providers. The guidelines would require implementation of several measures to strengthen the process of deployment and changes in application softwares in the ecosystem; continuous surveillance; implementation of controls on storage, processing and transmission of sensitive data; building capacity for forensic examination; and making the incident response mechanism more robust.

New Pre-Paid Payment Instruments (PPI)

Prepaid Payment Instruments (PPIs) have been playing an important role in promoting digital payments. To further facilitate its usage, it is proposed to introduce a new type of PPI which can be used only for purchase of goods and services up to a limit of ₹10,000. The loading/reloading of such PPI will be only from a bank account and used for making only digital payments such as bill payments, merchant payments, etc. Such PPIs can be issued on the basis of essential minimum details sourced from the customer.

*Detailed guidelines, where necessary will be issued by December 31, 2019.

Reserve Bank's Policy Perceptions I

"...... When interest rates and prices in general are set free, when real and financial markets are freed internally and interlinked globally, when the public sector will have to compete in a free market for the resources it requires, when, in fact, the economy aquires all the complexity and at least some of the sophistication of the richer countries, will we be still able to maintain the old baggage of a Quantity Theoretic frame of mind? Should inflation be the only area of concern in fiscal and monetary policy or should we also have to deal on occasion with unduly low investment and employment and untenable interest or exchange rates? Should we not then be familiar with the very great advances made in monetary economics in recent years both in theory and in ferreting out stable and meaningful relationships among a variety of strategic variables?......"

-I G Patel

(November 1993 in his Foreword to 'Monetary Economics for India' by Dr. Narendra Jadhav)

While India's central bank, like central banks elsewhere, is grappling with changing times, its recent efforts at tackling issues like virtual currencies, inflation, restoring confidence in banking and ethics in banking are nevertheless praiseworthy.

The First Bi-monthly Monetary Policy Statement, 2018–19 Resolution of the Monetary Policy Committee (MPC) Reserve Bank of India opened with a routine-looking statement:

"On the basis of an assessment of the current and evolving macroeconomic situation at its meeting today, the Monetary Policy Committee (MPC) decided to:

- keep the policy repo rate under the liquidity adjustment facility (LAF) unchanged at 6.0 per cent.

Consequently, the reverse repo rate under the LAF remains at 5.75 per cent, and the marginal standing facility (MSF) rate and the Bank Rate at 6.25 per cent."

A foot-note in small print said:

"From this resolution onwards, growth in gross domestic product (GDP) will be used as the headline measure of economic activity."

The shift from Gross Value Added (GVA) methodology to Gross Domestic Product (GDP)-based measure to compute growth estimates, stated to be to conform to international standards, was best explained by Deputy Governor Dr. Viral Acharya during a media interaction as under:

"Globally, the performance of most economies is gauged in terms of gross domestic product (GDP). This is also the approach followed by multilateral institutions, international analysts and investors, and primarily they all stick to this norms because it facilitates easy cross-country comparisons." While GVA gives a picture of the state of economic activity from the producers' side or supply side, the GDP model gives the picture from the consumers' side or demand perspective. On the face of it, the change looks rational.

Dr. Acharya observed that the Central Statistical Office (CSO) has started using GDP as the main measure of economic activities from this year.

Former Deputy Governor of RBI Ms. Usha Thorat, in her column in Business Line, identified 'a lower market borrowing programme with higher share of floaters and short term bonds, permission to spread the bond MTM provisions over the entire year and deferment of implementation of Indian Accounting Standards (Ind AS) by one year' as welcome positives and recalled Dr. Acharya's yet another thoughtful observation: "It is best for sake of policy credibility to not mix instruments with objectives they are not meant to target."

Reserve Bank of India in Limelight

The March 14, 2018 Ahmedabad speech of RBI Governor Urjit Patel sent out the message that the humility of central bankers is not indicative of the central bank's willingness to accept insults lying down. Arrogance of central banking is a time-tested antidote for several fiscal maladies.

The quote from I G Patel (1993) at the beginning of this chapter and Dr. Bimal Jalan's 2007 speech on "Ethics of Banking" (See Appendix XII for excerpts) are evidence enough to show that RBI had Governors with vision to see future and what was lacking in bringing about the changes they envisioned about reforming policies and procedures was, and is, the support from GOI which lack the will owing to political constraints.

> Since inception, Reserve Bank of India has been fortunate to have at its top, several eminent personalities who happened to be there, attracted not by the 'compensation package' or the opportunity to 'improve their CVs' for the next assignment, but by the challenges the institution provided to test their fitness for being associated with India's economic development. While making this observation, I have in mind Governors from Sir Osborne A Smith (1935–37) to Urjit Patel and several Deputy Governors including D R Mehta, R V Gupta, S S Tarapore, Rakesh Mohan and Viral Acharya. The number of Governors and Deputy Governors who were failures cannot go beyond that you can count on the fingers of one hand!

Arrogance of Central Banking

"The Humility of Central Bankers and the Arrogance of Central Banking" was the theme of S S Tarapore's address in a 'closed door interaction' at the RBI Auditorium, with his colleagues on September 30, 1996 the day he had retired as Deputy Governor (included as Chapter 16 in his book 'India's Monetary Policy in the Crucible of Reform' Vision Books, 2000). Excerpts:

"… We, in the Reserve Bank, need not be apologists for being zealous about inflation control. In fact, one should not be ashamed to be evangelical about our stance. As Dr. Manmohan Singh poignantly put it, inflation hurts the weakest segments of society the most and there can be no better anti-poverty programme than the control of inflation. Far from being defensive about our policy stance our critics must be told that excessive creation of money is a sure invitation to inflation and if hurting the poor is a sin then the advocates of a permissive monetary policy are the sinners of society. It is naïve to claim that we can kick-start the economy and that the printing press can generate output of steel, cement and machinery. It hardly needs to be stressed that excessive creation of money would merely result in inflation. We need not be overtly concerned by the esoteric punditry which claims to coax growth out of created money. Responding in 1979 to critics who argued that we need not take a squeamish or alarmist view of a sizeable increase in money supply, Dr. I G Patel, the then Governor with some element of agony said: "I am afraid this country of ours, great and blessed as it is, enjoys no such divine dispensation of immunity from monetary laws…"

Thus far about monetary policy and inflation. S S Tarapore also exhorted central banks to avoid three 'sins' in the same speech:

"… A central bank must strengthen its balance sheet as it can face very intense fluctuations which can have an adverse impact on its balance sheet and ultimately there is no one who can take care of the central bank if it mismanages its balance sheet. I have on earlier occasions referred to the "sins" of central banking and we must be arrogant enough to refuse to commit these sins. A central bank is a unique institution in the sense that it can expand or contract its balance sheet as a matter of deliberate policy and there is a danger that the central bank can be easily persuaded into imprudent policies. To briefly recapitulate these three sins are:

i. Automatic monetization of the budget deficit,

ii. Payment of interest on banks' cash balances with the central bank and

iii. The provision of various types of exchange risk guarantees……
Avoiding these three sins go to greatly strengthening the quality of the balance sheet of the Bank which is clearly of advantage to the economy as a whole…"

The quote is also in the context of GOI's exerting pressure on RBI to pay dividend on RBI's capital (which remains static at Rs. 5 crore since inception) on the basis of expectations expressed in union Budgets and the unusual open bargaining during FY2018 for advance transfer of 'surplus income' more than three months prior to June 30, 2018 (RBI's accounting year is July-June). RBI's reserves depleted to an all-time low, during the period 2013–16.

Currencies Outside the Monetary System

Reserve Bank of India recently made an observation that central banks around the world were exploring the option of introducing fiat digital currencies, keeping in view the rapid changes in the landscape of the payments industry along with factors such as emergence of private digital tokens and the rising costs of managing fiat paper/metallic money have led. Taking note that many central banks are still engaged in the debate, RBI constituted an interdepartmental group to study and provide guidance on the desirability and feasibility to introduce a central bank digital currency. An RBI notification had this to say on virtual currencies:

"Ring-fencing regulated entities from virtual currencies Technological innovations, including those underlying virtual currencies, have the potential to improve the efficiency and inclusiveness of the financial system. However, Virtual Currencies (VCs), also variously referred to as crypto currencies and crypto assets, raise concerns of consumer protection, market integrity and money laundering, among others. Reserve Bank has repeatedly cautioned users, holders and traders of virtual currencies, including Bitcoins, regarding various risks associated in dealing with such virtual currencies including Bitcoins, regarding various risks associated in dealing with such virtual currencies. In view of the associated risks, it has been decided that, with immediate effect, entities regulated by RBI shall not deal with or provide services to any individual or business entities dealing with or settling VCs. Regulated entities which already provide such services shall exit the relationship within a specified time."

As a follow-up RBI issued the following instructions to banks:

"Reserve Bank has repeatedly through its public notices on December 24, 2013, February 01, 2017 and December 05, 2017, cautioned users, holders and traders of virtual currencies, including Bitcoins, regarding various risks associated in dealing with such virtual currencies.

2. In view of the associated risks, it has been decided that, with immediate effect, entities regulated by the Reserve Bank shall not deal in VCs or provide services for facilitating any person or entity in dealing with or settling VCs. Such services include maintaining accounts, registering, trading, settling, clearing, giving loans against virtual tokens, accepting them as collateral, opening accounts of exchanges dealing with them and transfer/receipt of money in accounts relating to purchase/sale of VCs.

3. Regulated entities which already provide such services shall exit the relationship within three months from the date of this circular."

This move by RBI attracted mixed responses from media and analysts. Some termed it most retrograde. Let us read what Vaibhav Parikh and Arvind Ravindranath (both are lawyers with a law firm) said in an article published in Business Standard on April 10, 2018. The article opens with the following interesting observations:

"Strangely, the internet was also once feared as a product of technology. When the internet was new, criminals were the first ones to adopt it.

Believe it or not, there were calls to ban the internet. Once people realised the benefits of the internet, they focused on rooting out the criminal activity and not at banning the internet. It is for this reason that the Reserve Bank of India's (RBI) recent move can be termed its most retrograde."

Other comments by the learned lawyers include the scare about the possibility of only the legitimate players in the field (of virtual currency) getting affected, trade in the fast-growing virtual currency space moving overseas, tax evasion on account of transactions not going through banking channels and so on.

Appendix XII (Ref: Reserve Bank's Policy Perceptions I)

Ethics in Banking*

If rules of ethical behavior in banking were to be intrinsically dependent on ethical behavior in politics, or for that matter, in different segments of trade and commerce, then we are likely to be faced with an insoluble problem. Against this background, is there anything further that can be said specifically about ethics in banking, which is the subject of our discussion today?

I believe that, even after taking all the constraints into account, it is still possible to prescribe some rules of behavior which will make banking more ethical in developing countries, particularly in those countries which have an independent judiciary and an accountable administration. Let me move on to some prescriptive suggestions for promotion of ethics in banking for further consideration by central banks, experts and public in general.

The foremost requirement, in my view, to make our businesses, including banking, more ethical is to insist on standards of accounting and auditing which conform to the best international standards and ensure full financial disclosure. Banks, in particular, deal with other people's money. They are intermediary institutions which have been set up and licensed to accept deposits from the public, most of which are small in magnitude. They then lend such deposits to other users and producers for carrying out their business activities, which in turn are expected to generate employment and growth for the country as a whole. This intermediary function places a special responsibility on the banking sector. It is of utmost importance to ensure that there is complete transparency in respect of the use of depositors' money and ensuring safety of funds.

As the sub-prime crisis in the US and the UK has recently demonstrated, non-transparency and non-disclosure of financial obligations is not confined to developing countries alone. For all our countries, in the light of recent experience, it has become doubly important to revisit the banking, auditing and accounting standards and lay down guidelines which would ensure full disclosures of all obligations, including "off-balance-sheet" items.

One important ingredient of the proposed review of disclosure and accounting standards is to eliminate excessive secrecy that now prevails in regard to banking operations in many of our countries. I do not know enough about the situation in Bangladesh, but I know that in India, banks enjoy considerable legal protection in respect of disclosing identity of borrowers as well as defaults and rescheduling of outstanding payments. This non-disclosure is further buttressed by the Official Secrets Act, 1923, which protects government ministries and departments from disclosing anything in respect of formal or informal directions given by them to banks, regulatory authorities and other financial institutions. I see no reason why names and amounts lent by banks to individual borrowers should not be disclosed, and why even defaulters should enjoy the benefits of secrecy provisions.

The rationale for reducing the scope of secrecy provisions is to ensure that actions taken by banks conform to the normally accepted banking and regulatory guidelines, and are not unethical at least on the face of it. Public disclosure would also ensure some exercise of caution by banks in their lending operations, and in granting benefits to borrowers by way of rescheduling and so on. All such operations should not only be reasonable but also perceived to be so by the general public.

A difficult and somewhat thorny issue in regard to regulation and management of the banking sector is the role of politics in determining outcomes. In most developing countries, there is a strong view that banking and financial operations should be conducted to promote growth with equity, and special attention should be given to the poorer sections of the people in granting access to bank loans. In several countries, there are specific provisions in regard to quantum of lending that should be directed to persons below poverty line and certain other categories of borrowers. Since these provisions are meant to serve the interests of the people, peoples' representatives in Parliament and ministries claim to have a direct role in ensuring that banking operations conform to governmental priorities.

This view has substantial validity and must be respected as an important aspect of democratic accountability in developing countries. However, while ensuring public accountability for banking operations, it is equally important to ensure that political affiliations do not become the primary criterion for selection of top management or directors of banks. The objective of political neutrality in appointment of top management and directors can be met if the same processes are put in place for such selection as is presently the case for initial appointment of members in different civil services.

In several countries, civil servants are normally appointed through an open competitive examination process which is conducted by an independent institution, such as the Union Public Service Commission. There is no reason why a similar mechanism, at arm's length from the political executive, cannot be set up for the choice of top management and boards of directors in public sector banks. Selections can be made by an independent statutory Commission by inviting applications from qualified professionals and/or through appropriate search committees. The process for selection should be open and well-advertised. So far as private sector banks and other financial institutions are concerned, it is desirable for the government not to have any role in the selection process.

The point is simply that while financial priorities and banking policy may be decided at the political level, with due accountability, the political executive should not have any direct operational role in the choice of persons to run banks and other financial institutions. Such a process should ensure that, while there would always be some exceptions, the management and boards of banks are independent in their functioning and are not beholden to the changing political leadership for their appointments. (*Excerpts from the Speech by Dr. Bimal Jalan, Governor, RBI, at the 7th Nural Matin Memorial Lecture, Dhaka, July 20, 2007)

Reserve Bank's Policy Perceptions II

A mainstream financial newspaper editorial described Reserve Bank of India's August 1, 2018 monetary policy stance as "Ahead of the curve" (Business Standard, August 2, 2018). The media debate on the Bimonthly Monetary Policy Statement that followed did not go much beyond speculations on the consequences of base rate hike and, when the next rate hike can be expected. Suffice to say, one is tempted to doubt as to how many of those responsible for follow-up support needed for RBI to show results, read beyond the operational paragraphs in the Bimonthly Monetary Policy Statements and other documents like the minutes of each Monetary Policy Committee meeting issued religiously by RBI.

Banks have their own way of raising lending rates, irrespective of the real cost of resources or the guidance from the regulator. Since demonetization days, banks' dependence on RBI for funding credit has not been very high. If their resources come from deposits, common man expects a rise of at least 10 basis point increase in deposit rates across categories of deposits, when the cost of bank credit goes up by 20 basis points. Is this really happening? Even the Savings Bank deposit interest rate, after years of deregulation, has been stagnating around 4 percent per annum.

The reasons for MPC taking time to respond to market realities are many. This year, a fairly good monsoon has brought with it large scale losses also which will have an impact on government expenditure and market prices (read inflation). As most of the stakeholders including GOI, watch only for the end result, namely the change in base rate, of late, the responsibility of worrying about all factors affecting economic development is being shouldered by RBI. From climate change to the Fed Reserve's policy stance or political decisions affecting the health of the financial sector to pressures from FM for small change as 'interim dividend'!

One wishes, responses to the Monetary Policy Committee's bimonthly statements issued after two or three days' in-house deliberations by expert economists and central bankers are considered more seriously by policymakers and those who religiously criticize rate hikes. More importantly, all stakeholders need to reconcile to the reality that Monetary Policy tools presently under use by India's central bank will work only in a supportive environment, conducive to their operational efficiency, created by a healthy alignment of fiscal and monetary policies.

Urjit Patel, writing on monetary policy in a mainstream financial newspaper, more than ten years back ('RBI as an oil spigot,' Business Standard, September 3, 2008) gave some interesting insights on objectives of monetary policy and the tools used to achieve them by the central bank. I quote:

"Several conclusions and observations can be made. First, the dire fiscal situation the central government finds itself in has now sucked RBI in its vortex, but it is to be hoped that a durable alternative mechanism will be put in place with alacrity to ensure that the SMO (Special Market Operation) is not further resorted to; it can be argued that some of the hard work over the past decade to ensure that the RBI's proximate objective for conducting monetary policy is not compromised-by getting stuffed with government paper-has been undone. Second, we would be hard-pressed to name another country (even among that subsidize fuel) that has had to resort to the central bank in this manner. Third, praying for international crude prices to adjust sharply downwards soon does not constitute government's policy, sound or otherwise. Fourth, the proceeds of the oil bonds upon maturity will be in rupees, hence the RBI, if it wants to rebuild official foreign currency assets to make up for the decline on account of the SMO, will have to intervene in the market at the time and buy foreign currency at the ruling market exchange rate (the central bank shoulders an exchange rate risk if rebuilding foreign currency reserves is an objective)."

That was in 2008 and the background and context of monetary policy interventions are not the same today. After starting to work from Mint Road, with a research team comprising scores of Ph. Ds who have spent decades inside RBI to support, Dr. Patel's views on the dimensions of monetary policy and the instruments available must also have undergone changes. The difference between the RBI Governor in position in 2008 and Dr. Patel is, the latter has a team of chosen celebrity economists in the Monetary Policy Committee he chairs, to share the responsibility for RBI's policy stance announced bimonthly. This enables RBI to be more transparent and assertive about policy perceptions and the Governor better equipped to resist external pressures.

In this context, one remembers with gratitude the contribution of Dr. Raghuram Rajan to the evolution of MPC as a professional body it is today with a statutory backing. After the amendment to the Reserve Bank of India Act mandating RBI to chase inflation target, expectations from RBI are clear. According to Section 45 ZL of the amended RBI Act, 1934 the Reserve Bank shall publish, on the fourteenth day after every meeting of the Monetary Policy, the minutes of the proceedings of the meeting which shall include the following:

a. The resolution adopted at the meeting of the Monetary Policy Committee;

b. The vote of each member of the Monetary Policy Committee, ascribed to such member, on the resolution adopted in the said meeting; and

c. The statement of each member of the Monetary Policy Committee under sub-section (11) of section 45ZI on the resolution adopted in the said meeting.

To get a feel of the application of mind by members of MPC before voting for or against the final outcome of each meeting of the committee, one need to go through the minutes of meetings published on the fourteenth day after every meeting of the Monetary Policy Committee.

The Statement by MPC member Dr. Chetan Ghate at the eleventh meeting of the committee on June 4–6, 2018 is given in the Appendix XIII. Each of the six members of the MPC records justification for the position taken by them at the meeting in similar statements.

In a recent review of India under Article IV, International Monetary Fund (IMF) flagged external vulnerabilities on rising import bill, particularly from increasing oil prices and global protectionist measures.

The IMF has cautioned India against macro-financial risks which emerged from the government ownership of the public sector banks and suggested to the country that it should consider privatization of these lenders. Such suggestions, in my personal view, go beyond the brief of bodies like IMF, while the highlighting of the importance of a comprehensive plan to improve the governance, internal controls, and operations of public sector banks, should be accepted as constructive suggestions coming from an expert body. According to IMF, persistently-high household inflation expectations and large general government fiscal deficits and debt remain key macroeconomic challenges.

The IMF directors, who were responsible for the review, supported the recent tightening of monetary policy and the hike in repo rate announced in August must have given some comfort to the World Body.

Appendix XIII (Ref: Reserve Bank's Policy Perceptions II)

Excerpts from the minutes of the Monetary Policy Committee meeting held on June 4–6, 2018 (Source: RBI)

Statement by Dr. Chetan Ghate

Since the adoption of flexible inflation targeting in India (de facto in 2014 and de jure in 2016), the "great-disinflation" experienced by the Indian economy is a major accomplishment. After several years of high inflation in the run-up to 2014, the March 2018 CPI headline inflation (ex-HRA) rate of 3.9% is a testimony to the successful conduct of monetary policy given its consistency with the 4 +/− 2 percent target recommended by the Urjit Patel Committee report in 2014 and enshrined in the Reserve Bank of India Act, 1934 in 2016. Both the Reserve Bank of India and the Government of India should be congratulated in calibrating a monetary-fiscal mix that has helped engender this disinflation. Good luck helped with this outcome but so did good policy.

Inflation targeting however can truly become successful if the inflation target and the inflation forecast become identical on a durable basis. Locking in the 4 percent medium target therefore requires continual vigilance.

Since the last review, demand conditions have continued to remain robust. Q4: 2017–2018 headline growth of 7.7% was the highest in 7 quarters. While capacity utilization increased throughout 2017–18, the pick-up since Q3 (74.1%) appears to be decisive. The successful resolution of cases under the Insolvency and Bankruptcy Code will further assist capacity utilization without requiring new investment.

Despite the PMIs for services being somewhat fragile, overall corporate profits remain strong. While consumption (PFCE) growth remains tepid (the Q4 growth print was close to the average of the last 7 quarters), the strong revival of investment demand, manufacturing, and construction gives me more confidence about the durability of the growth recovery. Even though the high growth print of Q4:2017–2018 is pushed up by a base effect, I am more certain that the ongoing cyclical recovery in growth will sustain and this will lead to a faster closing of the output gap.

The revival of growth brings new inflationary risks that need to be carefully watched. The RBI's enterprise surveys suggest that upward pressures in input and staff costs are being marked by an increase in selling prices. Staff costs in services increased by 6.6%, and 11.6% in manufacturing compared to the last round of the survey. Food inflation continues to be maverick with a 4th consecutive month decline: the usual seasonal uptick in April uncharacteristically surprised on the downside. CPI inflation ex food and fuel, which in April, sustained close to 6%, with strong momentum effects is worryingly becoming the main driver of inflation. Almost all components of CPI ex food fuel registered upticks suggesting that demand-pull forces are creeping into CPI headline inflation.

A major upside risk to the one-year ahead CPI projections has been the price of oil. This has been on a durable rise over the past six months, reflecting stronger global growth and the increasing costs of creating capacity in substitutes. While a strong dollar and the price of oil usually follows an inverse relationship, the usual "coupling" has been confounded by geo-political events in recent months. The volatility in the price of oil needs to be carefully watched, especially because higher fuel prices have helped harden inflationary expectations (both the 3- month ahead and 1-year ahead) to their highest level since September 2016.

The combination of cost-push and demand-pull factors at the current juncture has put one-year ahead inflation projections significantly above 4%. This warrants a monetary policy response. However, because of uncertainty surrounding the price of oil, and the nascent recovery of the economy, it would be opportune to take small steps.

I await details on the MSP policy. The outcome of a simultaneous twin terms of trade shock to the Indian economy as explained in my minutes of the April MPC meeting needs to be carefully watched.

I vote for an increase in the policy repo rate by 25 basis points at today's meeting of the Monetary Policy Committee.

Rating RBI's Policy: Beyond Rate Cuts

Reserve Bank of India, supported by a majority decision (4–2) of the Monetary Policy Committee (MPC), on February 7, 2019, decided to reduce the Repo rate by 25 basis points, down from 6.5 percent to 6.25 percent. Mainstream financial dailies next day hailed the decision with headlines like, "RBI Cuts Repo 25 bps, Softer Rate Regime on the Horizon" calling it a big surprise. The Repo rate which was at 8 percent in January 2014 had been gradually brought down to 6 percent in August 2017 and had been raised to 6.25 percent in June and 6.5 percent in August 2018.

The 25 basis point reduction in Repo Rate works out to just 4 percent reduction in the rate. Banking system is at present availing a negligible percentage of their total resources needs from RBI. This explains the poor impact of changes in base rates on lending/deposit rates.

The intention is not to underestimate the good work being done by the MPC since it has started working with statutory backing and holds bi-monthly three days meetings before giving shape to the policy stance each time. The purpose is to highlight the relevance of the process and content of MPC deliberations which penetrate into the entire structure of Indian Economy, much beyond the decision on base rates.

The myth that MPC has two teams representing GOI and RBI has also been broken this time, as a 'GOI nominee' and one RBI Deputy Governor on the Committee did not go with the majority decision to cut rates. The MPC's vote to shift the monetary policy stance from calibrated tightening to neutral was, however, unanimous.

The announcement says:

"The decision to change the monetary policy stance was unanimous. As regards the reduction in the policy repo rate, Dr. Ravindra H. Dholakia, Dr. Pami Dua, Dr. Michael Debabrata Patra and Shri Shaktikanta Das voted in favour of the decision. Dr. Chetan Ghate and Dr. Viral V. Acharya voted to keep the policy rate unchanged. The MPC reiterates its commitment to achieving the medium-term target for headline inflation of 4 per cent on a durable basis."

Taking into account fiscal risk, demand pressures, high core inflation and uncertain oil prices, MPC could have kept rates on hold while changing stance. Where was the hurry for the MPC to announce to the world that there is a policy 'U' turn, with the exit of Urjit Patel? Let us wait for the minutes of the MPC meeting which will be published after a fortnight from February 7, 2019. Dr. Chetan Ghate and Dr. Viral Acharya may have some points to make.

Usually, the post-Monetary Policy Review debates hover around the repo rate and inflation. All stakeholders have started thinking about the relevance of RBI in taking forward economic reforms and the need to ensure that the central bank stays on in one piece to be available to defend monetary and fiscal policies which get hijacked for extraneous considerations. It is in this context one observes with comfort the present change in the approach of media and analysts to take cognizance of the multiple ingredients of the Bi-monthly policy review exercise RBI has been doing ritualistically as part of its mandated responsibility. Perhaps, this change to go into small print is one of the welcome byproducts of the forced exit of Urjit Patel. Another outcome is the recognition that public spar over differences in policy perception or veiled threats to invoke provisions like those in Section 7 of the RBI Act which are there for different purposes, to discipline RBI Governor do not serve any useful purpose. It has to be said to the credit of GOI at the highest level, that, rising to the occasion, the crisis arising from the abrupt disappearance of Urjit Patel was resolved within 24 hours by appointing an equally competent person Shri Shaktikanta Das, who didn't need much familiarization about the 'functions and working' of India's central bank, to take RBI forward from where Patel had left.

State Bank of India chairman Rajnish Kumar profusely praised the February 7 monetary policy statement describing it as 'rich in content and pronounced in communication.' In reality, the description would go well with at least the preceding four bi-monthly announcements. The problem was, many ignored the real content of the policy announcement read with the statements on regulatory and supervisory policy measures (which are now being simultaneously released with monetary policy announcements) and concentrated on the changes in base rates.

Rajnish Kumar, writing in Mint made the following observations which are indicative of the deeper interest the stakeholders have started showing in the direction the RBI's policy is moving:

"The policy guidance is also guided by the fact that the global growth outlook has become more uncertain. Among key advanced nations, economic activity in the US lost some steam while in the Euro area, economic activity has lost momentum on weak industrial activity. Commodity prices, including base metal prices, are showing mixed trends. The internal growth signals are also indicating minor moderation in services. Thus, policy accommodation at this juncture was warranted to balance both internal and external growth sources. The fiscal measures provided in the interim budget have bolstered the growth outlook for FY20 at 7.4%. The rate cut of 25 basis points will support the overall growth trajectory, both through investments and private consumption.

This policy should perhaps be appreciated more for its development and regulatory proposals, since such steps could trigger a paradigm shift in the financial markets in terms of new understanding and thinking among market participants."

RBI's conscious efforts to be more transparent in communication was evident in the press briefing Team RBI had immediately after policy announcement (Appendix XIV) and the online media interaction on the same day.

Plea to Retain the Institutional Strength of RBI

Former RBI Deputy Governor Usha Thorat speaking at Stella Maris College for Women, covered the evolution of RBI as a 'full service central bank' making the institution different from other central banks in the world which carry out mostly core central banking functions. She had this to say about central bank's policy and financial independence:

"With regard to goal independence, the preamble to the RBI Act was amended in 2016 to give statutory status to the Monetary Policy Committee (MPC), and to mandate inflation targeting as the primary objective of India's monetary policy framework. This move implemented the recommendations of the various committees mentioned earlier and has been widely welcomed as a major monetary policy reform. The Act says that the Central Government shall, in consultation with the Bank, determine the inflation target in terms of the Consumer Price Index, once in every five years. This gives the Reserve Bank of India operational independence while the goal is set by the elected government. Recognizing the difficulties involved in narrow inflation targeting for India, the actual range of 2–6% for CPI inflation set in the March 2015 agreement is quite wide and allows for flexibility. The main advantage with having an explicit target is that it sets inflationary expectations, which itself is a factor affecting inflation. Accountability is enshrined in the Act, as there will need to be a report in the case of not adhering to the target.

From the point of financial independence, the Fiscal Responsibility Act that prohibits RBI participation in the primary market is critical in ensuring that there is no fiscal dominance. In the case of the public debt management, there can be no independence and there has always been close coordination between the RBI and the MOF. Another aspect of financial independence is in terms of the transfer of profits to the Government each year. For several years RBI built up internal reserves to ensure that these are commensurate with the growth in the balance sheet. In the recent period, all surplus profits have been transferred on grounds that the capital is adequate based on a risk management model adopted by the RBI. This has led to a reduction in the ratio of the contingency reserve to the total assets of RBI. This is the cushion available to RBI in its balance sheet to ensure flexibility in policy making."

It cannot be just coincidence that former RBI governor Dr. Y V Reddy chose the subject "Central Banking in India: Retrospect and

Prospects" for his 'Kale Memorial lecture 2018 delivered at Gokhale Institute of Politics and Economics Pune on February 8, 2019. In a fairly long speech, Dr. Reddy has given a recap of the history of central banking in the Indian context and traced the evolution of RBI to its present status. Referring to the present MPC dispensation, he said:

"The monetary policy framework in India has to be operated by the Reserve Bank of India, and the regime is described as flexible inflation targetting. The central government under the new framework determines the inflation target in terms of consumer price index once in five years. It appoints a Monetary Policy Committee consisting of three members including the Governor from the RBI, and three outside experts nominated by the government through a procedure prescribed under the law."

Dr. Reddy's observations on current challenges faced by RBI needs immediate attention of GOI and RBI. I quote a portion specifically relevant to the strength of RBI, from the speech:

"Current Issues – 2019:

In October 2018, it transpired that Government had sought the opinions of the Governor under Section 7 in order to give directions to the RBI in public interest. This is unprecedented and virtually meant that the channels of normal communication for reaching agreed position between Government and Governor RBI had broken down. The Board of RBI appeared to have differences with Governor on the same issues. These differences came into public domain after a speech by a Deputy Governor.

The Central Bank's Deputy Governor, Viral Acharya gave a landmark speech in October 2018, in which he virtually warned the Government that undermining RBI's independence would attract the wrath of the markets. The speech provoked strong response from the government which interpreted the Deputy Governor's speech – a speech that was admittedly authorised by the Governor, and represents institutional position, as an act defiance rather than as an expression of disagreement with the Government. It triggered a prolonged war of words between the Deputy Governor RBI and Secretary Economic Affairs, Ministry of Finance, but this subsided with the departure of Urjit Patel in December. The resolution of issues originally flagged for consideration under Section 7 are likely to impact the future role of RBI as evident from debates nationwide on autonomy of Reserve bank of India. It is interesting that the market reactions to the proposals of RBI have not been as severe or as depressing as it was made out in Acharya's speech presumably because both financial market and Governments have a short term bias. expression of disagreement with the Government. It triggered a prolonged war of words between the Deputy Governor RBI and Secretary Economic Affairs, Ministry of Finance, but this subsided with the departure of Urjit Patel in December, 2018. The resolution of issues originally flagged for consideration under Section 7 are likely to impact the future role of RBI as evident from debates nationwide on autonomy of Reserve bank of India. It is interesting that the market reactions to the proposals of RBI have not been as severe or as depressing as it was made out in Acharya's speech presumably because both financial market and Governments have a short term bias.

First and foremost contentious issue relates to the use of excess reserves in the balance sheet of RBI. This is not the first attempt by the Government in this regard. In 1986, Government demanded RBI's profits in the Government's quest for fiscal relief. Governor Malhotra explained how the profits of RBI were different from the normal profits of other public sector companies, and added that they were notional. He explained that higher transfers would impact the economy adversely and made it clear that the profits of RBI should not be considered as an avenue for augmenting the resources of the Government.

During the reform period till 2013, the Government took several steps to strengthen the balance sheet of Reserve Bank of India and added to the reserves. For instance, the excessive cost of sterilisation which normally is borne by the Central bank was shared by the Government to keep the Central bank strong to be able to serve the Government better in times of difficulties. In recent years, the Government has reviewed this approach. Further, by taking recourse to unprecedented practice of interim dividend, the spirit of limit on Ways and Means arrangement under fiscal management legislation has been compromised. The immediate fiscal needs seem to take precedence over a renewed assessment of the capital needs of RBI.

In 2018 the Government took the stand that the existing levels of reserves are in excess of the requirement and, therefore, the excess of reserves could be legitimately claimed for use by the Government. Government was laying claim to stock and not merely flow. In its calculation, the government took into account the revaluation gains on forex assets on account of depreciation of the rupee over the years. RBI, on the other hand, took the view that the reserves are not in excess and that, even if they were in excess, the purpose will be served over the years by sticking to the legal requirement of transferring to its reserves a portion of the current surplus of income over expenditure till the reserves need to be augmented. The Chief Economic Adviser had already proposed that the excess of reserves should be made available for injecting capital to the public sector banks which are currently under-capitalised.

The law and the current practice are for the Board to determine on a yearly basis the excess of income over expenditure, the amount required for addition to its reserves and then the residual is transferred to the Government as dividends. This surplus thus flows to the Consolidated Fund of India for use as it deems fit. As part of the reforms, a formula was approved by the Board for transfer of such reserves and remained in force till 2014. However, the Government took the position that the level of reserves of RBI are in excess of needs and that the entire surplus of income over expenditure should be transferred to the Government. This was done in the year 2015.

There is no doubt that in the ultimate analysis, the Government as the owner has a claim over the reserves, but the way it exercises gives signals to the market and influences public opinion. In law, the Board will have to decide on this, and the Board members are nominated by the government. There are two substantive issues. One is determination of excess reserves and whether this should only be confined to realised gains or can apply to revaluation gains as well, and the second issue is the immediate use of excess reserves, as determined.

There are different approaches to the level of capital of a central bank. One view is that Government will provide support to it when needed and hence issue of adequacy does not arise. All income over expenditure every year could get transferred to Government. Alternatively the government may like to assure the markets that its Central bank has the Capital to meet contingencies that may arise without depending on governments. There is merit in keeping at least central bank's balance sheet strong if the Government's fiscal balance sheet is weak. But substantively, it is the judgement of Government that prevails on the adequacy issues though procedurally that of Board.

Use of reserves accumulated in the past will have to consider three factors, namely, a) the macroeconomic implications of such transfers, in particular, the monetary implications which are likely to be expansive; b) the issues of inter generational equity since the reserves have been accumulated as an Insurance for the future; c) the constitutional propriety of using the reserves directly to fund capital of the banks instead of crediting it to Consolidated Fund of India and then using it as considered necessary by the Government, and d) the incongruity of the banking regulator being asked to use its resources to fund banks that are in need of the capital. A Committee has been appointed to advise the RBI on the capital framework and related matters."

Appendix XIV (Ref: Rating RBI's Policy: Beyond Rate Cuts)

Opening remarks by RBI Governor Shaktikanta Das at the press briefing that followed the Monetary Policy Announcement on February 07, 2019

Over the past two and a half days i.e., during February 5,6 and 7, 2019 the Monetary Policy Committee (MPC) reviewed the macroeconomic and financial conditions and prospects and voted by a 4/2 majority to reduce the policy repo rate by 25 basis points. The MPC also voted unanimously to shift the monetary policy stance from calibrated tightening to neutral. I would like to take this opportunity to thank the MPC members for their extremely valuable contributions, and the richness and high quality of the discussions that we had. I also would like to thank our teams in the Reserve Bank who provided inputs and support at various stages of policy formulation. Let me begin by setting out key developments that the MPC considered while arriving at the policy decision. The MPC noted that global growth is slowing down across key advanced economies (AEs) and in some major emerging market economies (EMEs) as well. World trade is also losing momentum. While international commodity prices, especially of crude, have recovered from their December lows, they remain soft. In consonance, inflation has edged down in major AEs and many EMEs. Global financial markets have regained poise from heightened turbulence in December, with equity markets paring earlier losses, bond yields easing and EME currencies appreciating, aided by a weaker US dollar. As regards domestic macroeconomic developments, the MPC noted that the CSO has placed India's real GDP growth at 7.2 per cent in 2018–19, with gross fixed capital formation (GFCF) accelerating, but consumption expenditure moderating and net exports improving. More recent high frequency indicators point to investment demand losing some pace in the third quarter of 2018–19, while credit flows to industry remain muted. On the supply side, output from agriculture and allied activities and services is expected by the CSO to decelerate in 2018–19. Rabi sowing up to February 1, 2019 has been lower than in the previous year, but it could catch up in the remaining part of the sowing season. The extended period of cold weather in this year's winter is also likely to boost wheat yields. In the industrial sector, activity measured by the index of industrial production (IIP) slowed down in November, even as capacity utilisation in the manufacturing sector increased above trend. Survey-based indicators point to weakening of demand conditions in the manufacturing sector. High-frequency indicators of the services sector suggest some moderation in the pace of activity. In its assessment of inflation developments, the MPC noted that headline CPI inflation declined to 2.2 per cent in December, the lowest print in the last eighteen months. Continuing deflation in food items, a sharp fall in fuel inflation and some edging down of inflation, excluding food and fuel, contributed to the decline in headline inflation. Moreover, inflation expectations of households have softened by 80 basis points for the three-months' ahead horizon and by 130 basis points for the twelve-month horizon. Producers assess that inflation in prices of farm inputs and industrial raw materials eased in Q3 while growth in rural wages moderated. On the external front, export growth was almost flat while import growth slowed in November and turned negative in December 2018. Consequently, the merchandise trade deficit for April-December 2018 was a shade higher than its level a year ago, although higher services exports and low oil prices should have a salutary impact on the current account deficit in Q3. On the financing side, net FDI inflows to India during April-November 2018 were higher than a year ago. Foreign portfolio flows turned negative in January 2019, after rebounding in November and December 2018. India's foreign exchange reserves were at US$ 400.2 billion on February 1, 2019. Turning to the outlook, the MPC took into consideration these developments and revised the path of CPI inflation downwards to 2.8 per cent in Q4:2018–19, 3.2–3.4 per cent in H1:2019–20 and 3.9 per cent in Q3:2019–20, with risks broadly balanced around the central trajectory. GDP growth for 2019–20 is projected at 7.4 per cent – in the range of 7.2–7.4 per cent in H1, and 7.5 per cent in Q3 – with risks evenly balanced. It is noteworthy that the path of inflation has moved downwards significantly, and over the period of the next one year, headline inflation is expected to remain contained below or at its target of 4 per cent. This has opened up space for policy action. Meanwhile investment activity is recovering but supported mainly by public spending on infrastructure. The need is to strengthen private investment activity. Private consumption also needs to be buttressed. While bank credit flows have picked up and overall flows to the commercial sector have also picked up, they are yet to become broad-based. The favourable macroeconomic configuration that is evolving underscores the need to act now when it is most opportune. In pursuance of the provisions of the RBI Act as amended in 2016, it is vital to act decisively and in a timely manner to address the objective of growth once the objective of price stability as defined in the Act is achieved. The shift in the stance of monetary policy from calibrated tightening to neutral also provides flexibility and the room to address challenges to sustained growth of the Indian economy over the coming months, as long as the inflation outlook remains benign. The decisions of the MPC in this regard will be data driven and in consonance with the primary objective of monetary policy to maintain price stability while keeping in mind the objective of growth. Now let me turn to some developmental and regulatory policies that have been announced, which complement the monetary policy stance and action. Several measures are being proposed in areas spanning financial markets, regulation of banks and non-banking financial companies (NBFCs), regulation of payment and settlement systems and financial inclusion in the Statement on Developmental and Regulatory Polices, i.e., Part B of the Monetary Policy Statement. These policy actions will be anchored by the goal of financial stability, so that the soundness and efficiency of the financial system in intermediating the economy's needs of financial resources for productive purposes is preserved at all costs. With regard to financial markets, i. the Reserve Bank proposes to modify the foreign exchange derivative regulations, i.e., Regulation FEMA-25, in order to improve access and participation by promoting operational ease and removing regulatory differentiation based on residence, product and type of transaction; ii. a task force on offshore rupee markets will assess the causes underlying the growth of this market and recommend measures to encourage non-residents to access the domestic market; iii. interest rate derivative directions would be rationalised with the objective of simplifying regulations and reducing prescriptive stipulations to promote liquidity by encouraging participation, product innovation and by easing access norms; iv. a draft regulation of financial benchmarks is proposed, which is based on the practices recommended by international standard setting bodies and lays down governance, quality and accountability standards for administrators of 'significant' benchmarks in the markets regulated by the Reserve Bank; v. the provision that no foreign portfolio investor (FPI) shall have exposure of more than 20 per cent of its corporate bond portfolio to a single corporate is being withdrawn to encourage a wider spectrum of investors to access the Indian debt market; and vi. resolution applicants under IBC will be permitted to avail external commercial borrowings under the approval route to lower their cost of funding for repaying outstanding rupee loans availed by the companies undergoing the Corporate Insolvency Resolution Process(CIRP) – this is expected to improve the overall effectiveness of this process. Proposals relating to regulation of banks and NBFCs include i. revising the definition of 'bulk deposit" as a single rupee deposit of '₹2 crore and above' instead of the earlier threshold of '₹1 crore and above' in order to provide greater operational flexibility to banks in raising such deposits; ii. establishment of an Umbrella Organisation for urban co-operative banks (UCBs) that can provide several services so as to enhance public confidence in the UCB sector, provide regulatory comfort and promote financial stability in an inter-connected financial system; iii. harmonisation of three separate categories of NBFCs viz., Asset Finance Companies, Loan Companies and Investment Companies (which together constitute almost 99 per cent of NBFCs in terms of numbers) by creating a merged category called NBFC – Investment and Credit Company (NBFC-ICC), in order to address the complexities associated with multiple categories of NBFCs and to provide the NBFCs greater flexibility in their operations which would result in diversified product offerings, and better access to NBFI services; iv. alignment of risk weights of bank exposures to all categories of NBFCs, other than CICs, with their credit ratings, with a view to facilitating credit flow to better rated NBFCs, lowering the cost of bank borrowings for NBFCs and in turn, for end consumers, particularly borrowers of MFIs. Proposals related to enhancing financial inclusion include two points: i. Enhancing the limit of collateral free agriculture loans from ₹1 lakh to ₹1.6 lakh, keeping in view the overall increase in inflation and rise in agriculture input costs –

this is expected to enhance coverage of farmers in getting access to formal credit; ii. Setting up of an internal working group to examine and recommend measures to address issues pertaining to the policy framework and delivery of agricultural credit in the country. On the payment systems, the feasibility of bringing payment related activities of Payment Gateway Service Providers and Payment Aggregators under the direct regulatory ambit of the Reserve Bank will be examined. This is considered necessary given their increasing importance in the evolving structure of payment systems in the country and the fact that at present, they are essentially regulated indirectly through the banks with whom they have a tie-up. Thank you. We will now take questions.

RBI's Monetary Policy: In the Right Direction

All stakeholders need to reconcile to the reality that Monetary Policy tools presently under use by India's central bank will work only in a supportive environment, conducive to their operational efficiency, created by a healthy alignment of fiscal and monetary policies.

A mainstream financial newspaper editorial described Reserve Bank of India's August 1, 2018 monetary policy stance as "Ahead of the curve." The media debate that followed on the latest Bimonthly Monetary Policy Statement did not go much beyond speculations on the consequences of base rate hike and, when the next rate hike can be expected. Suffice to say, one is tempted to doubt as to how many of those responsible for follow-up support needed for RBI to show results, read beyond the operational paragraphs in the Bimonthly Monetary Policy Statements and other documents like the minutes of each Monetary Policy Committee meeting issued religiously by RBI.

Banks have their own way of raising lending rates, irrespective of the real cost of resources or the guidance from the regulator. Since demonetization days, banks' dependence on RBI for funding credit has not been very high. If their resources come from deposits, common man expects a rise of at least 10 basis point increase in deposit rates across categories of deposits, when the cost of bank credit goes up by 20 basis points. Is this really happening? Even the Savings Bank deposit interest rate, after years of deregulation, has been stagnating around 4 percent per annum.

The reasons for MPC taking time to respond to market realities are many. Most of the years, when we get a fairly good monsoon, large scale losses due to crop-loss and damages to infrastructure also follow due to floods etc which will have an impact on government expenditure and market prices of agricultural produce. As most of the stakeholders including GOI, watch only for the end result, namely the change in base rate, of late, the responsibility of worrying about all factors affecting economic development is being shouldered by RBI. From climate change to the Fed Reserve's policy stance or political decisions affecting the health of the financial sector to pressures from FM for small change as 'interim dividend'!

One wishes, responses to MPC's (Monetary Policy Committee's) bimonthly statements issued after two or three days' in-house deliberations by expert economists and central bankers are considered more seriously by policymakers and those who criticize rate hikes. More importantly, all stakeholders need to reconcile to the reality that Monetary Policy tools presently under use by India's central bank will work only in a supportive environment, conducive to their operational efficiency, created by a healthy alignment of fiscal and monetary policies.

Present RBI Governor Urjit Patel, writing on monetary policy in a mainstream financial newspaper, some ten years back ('RBI as an oil spigot,' Business Standard, September 3, 2008) gave some interesting insights on objectives of monetary policy and the tools used to achieve them by the central bank. I quote:

"Several conclusions and observations can be made. First, the dire fiscal situation the central government finds itself in has now sucked RBI in its vortex, but it is to be hoped that a durable alternative mechanism will be put in place with alacrity to ensure that the SMO (Special Market Operation) is not further resorted to; it can be argued that some of the hard work over the past decade to ensure that the RBI's proximate objective for conducting monetary policy is not compromised-by getting stuffed with government paper-has been undone. Second, we would be hard-pressed to name another country (even among that subsidize fuel) that has had to resort to the central bank in this manner. Third, praying for international crude prices to adjust sharply downwards soon does not constitute government's policy, sound or otherwise. Fourth, the proceeds of the oil bonds upon maturity will be in rupees, hence the RBI, if it wants to rebuild official foreign currency assets to make up for the decline on account of the SMO, will have to intervene in the market at the time and buy foreign currency at the ruling market exchange rate (the central bank shoulders an exchange rate risk if rebuilding foreign currency reserves is an objective)."

That was in 2008 and the background and context of monetary policy interventions are not the same today. After starting to work from Mint Road, with a research team of scores of Ph. Ds who have spent decades inside RBI to support, Dr. Patel's views on the dimensions of monetary policy and the instruments available must also have undergone change during the recent years. The difference between the RBI Governor in position in 2008 and Dr. Patel is, the latter has a team of chosen celebrity economists in the Monetary Policy Committee he chairs, to share the responsibility for RBI's policy stance announced bimonthly. This enables RBI to be more transparent assertive about policy perceptions and the Governor more equipped to resist external pressures.

We should remember with gratitude the contribution of Dr. Raghuram Rajan to the evolution of MPC as a professional body it is today with a statutory backing. After the amendment to the Reserve Bank of India Act mandating RBI to chase inflation target, expectations from RBI are clear. According to Section 45 ZL of the amended RBI Act, 1934 the Reserve Bank shall publish, on the fourteenth day after every meeting of the Monetary Policy, the minutes of the proceedings of the meeting which shall include the following, namely:–

a. The resolution adopted at the meeting of the Monetary Policy Committee;

b. The vote of each member of the Monetary Policy Committee, ascribed to such member, on the resolution adopted in the said meeting; and

c. The statement of each member of the Monetary Policy Committee under sub-section (11) of section 45ZI on the resolution adopted in the said meeting.

To get a feel of the application of mind by members of MPC before voting for or against the final outcome of each meeting of the committee, one can go through the minutes of each meeting published on the fourteenth day after every meeting of the Monetary Policy Committee. The Statement by MPC member Dr. Chetan Ghate at the eleventh meeting of the committee on June 4–6, 2018 is given in the Appendix XV. Each of the six members of the MPC records justification for the position he takes at the meeting in similar statements.

IMF Review

In its recent review of India under Article IV, International Monetary Fund (IMF) flagged external vulnerabilities on rising import bill, particularly from increasing oil prices and global protectionist measures.

The IMF has cautioned India against macro-financial risks which emerged from the government ownership of the public sector banks and suggested to the country that it should consider privatization of these lenders. Such suggestions, in my personal view, go beyond the brief of bodies like IMF, while the highlighting of the importance of a comprehensive plan to improve the governance, internal controls, and operations of public sector banks, should be accepted as constructive suggestions coming from an expert body. According to IMF, persistently-high household inflation expectations and large general government fiscal deficits and debt remain key macro-economic challenges.

The IMF directors, who were responsible for the review, supported the recent tightening of monetary policy in June 2018 and the hike in repo rate announced in August must have given some comfort to the World Body.

Appendix XV (Ref: RBI's Monetary Policy: In the Right Direction)

Excerpts from the minutes of the Monetary Policy Committee meeting held on June 4–6, 2018

Statement by Dr. Chetan Ghate

Since the adoption of flexible inflation targeting in India (de facto in 2014 and de jure in 2016), the "great-disinflation" experienced by the Indian economy is a major accomplishment. After several years of high inflation in the run-up to 2014, the March 2018 CPI headline inflation (ex-HRA) rate of 3.9% is a testimony to the successful conduct of monetary policy given its consistency with the 4 +/− 2 percent target recommended by the Urjit Patel Committee report in 2014 and enshrined in the Reserve Bank of India Act, 1934 in 2016. Both the Reserve Bank of India and the Government of India should be congratulated in calibrating a monetary-fiscal mix that has helped engender this disinflation. Good luck helped with this outcome but so did good policy.

Inflation targeting however can truly become successful if the inflation target and the inflation forecast become identical on a durable basis. Locking in the 4 percent medium target therefore requires continual vigilance.

Since the last review, demand conditions have continued to remain robust. Q4: 2017- 2018 headline growth of 7.7% was the highest in 7 quarters. While capacity utilization increased throughout 2017–18, the pick-up since Q3 (74.1%) appears to be decisive. The successful resolution of cases under the Insolvency and Bankruptcy Code will further assist capacity utilization without requiring new investment.

Despite the PMIs for services being somewhat fragile, overall corporate profits remain strong. While consumption (PFCE) growth remains tepid (the Q4 growth print was close to the average of the last 7 quarters), the strong revival of investment demand, manufacturing, and construction gives me more confidence about the durability of the growth recovery. Even though the high growth print of Q4:2017–2018 is pushed up by a base effect, I am more certain that the ongoing cyclical recovery in growth will sustain and this will lead to a faster closing of the output gap.

The revival of growth brings new inflationary risks that need to be carefully watched. The RBI's enterprise surveys suggest that upward pressures in input and staff costs are being marked by an increase in selling prices. Staff costs in services increased by 6.6%, and 11.6% in manufacturing compared to the last round of the survey. Food inflation continues to be maverick with a 4th consecutive month decline: the usual seasonal uptick in April uncharacteristically surprised on the downside. CPI inflation ex food and fuel, which in April, sustained close to 6%, with strong momentum effects is worryingly becoming the main driver of inflation. Almost all components of CPI ex food fuel registered upticks suggesting that demand-pull forces are creeping into CPI headline inflation.

A major upside risk to the one-year ahead CPI projections has been the price of oil. This has been on a durable rise over the past six months, reflecting stronger global growth and the increasing costs of creating capacity in substitutes. While a strong dollar and the price of oil usually follows an inverse relationship, the usual "coupling" has been confounded by geo-political events in recent months. The volatility in the price of oil needs to be carefully watched, especially because higher fuel prices have helped harden inflationary expectations (both the 3- month ahead and 1-year ahead) to their highest level since September 2016.

The combination of cost-push and demand-pull factors at the current juncture has put one-year ahead inflation projections significantly above 4%. This warrants a monetary policy response. However, because of uncertainty surrounding the price of oil, and the nascent recovery of the economy, it would be opportune to take small steps.

I await details on the MSP policy. The outcome of a simultaneous twin terms of trade shock to the Indian economy as explained in my minutes of the April MPC meeting needs to be carefully watched.

I vote for an increase in the policy repo rate by 25 basis points at today's meeting of the Monetary Policy Committee.

Monetary Policy II: RBI Takes Charge

PREAMBLE of the Reserve Bank of India mandates the central bank "to regulate the issue of Bank notes and the keeping of reserves with a view to securing monetary stability in [2] [India] and generally to operate the currency and credit system of the country to its advantage"

Prior to the establishment of the Reserve Bank, the Indian financial system was totally inadequate on account of the inherent weakness of the dual control of currency by the Central Government and of credit by the Imperial Bank of India.

The Hilton-Young Commission, therefore, recommended that the dichotomy of functions and division of responsibility for control of currency and credit and the divergent policies in this respect must be ended by setting-up of a central bank – called the Reserve Bank of India – which would regulate the financial policy and develop banking facilities throughout the country. Hence, the Bank was established with this primary object in view.

Another objective of the Reserve Bank has been to remain free from political influence and be in successful operation for maintaining financial stability and credit. The fundamental object of the Reserve Bank of India is to discharge purely central banking functions in the Indian money market, i.e., to act as the note-issuing authority, bankers' bank and banker to government, and to promote the growth of the economy within the framework of the general economic policy of the Government, consistent with the need of maintenance of price stability.

A significant object of the Reserve Bank of India has also been to assist the planned process of development of the Indian economy. Besides the traditional central banking functions, with the launching of the five-year plans in the country, the Reserve Bank of India has been moving ahead in performing a host of developmental and promotional functions, which are normally beyond the purview of a traditional Central Bank.

The above background becomes relevant in the context of certain unprecedented developments like retail inflation overshooting the given target of 4 (+)/(-) 2 percent being chased by RBI by more than one percent and RBI experimenting new alternatives for improving liquidity in the system and being transparent in seeking fiscal policy support while doing its best in policy areas where the central bank is in charge. To be factual, retail inflation was. 7.59 percent for January 2020, higher by 24 basis points from 7.35 percent reached in the previous month. MPC sees CPI inflation at 6.5 percent for January–March 2020 and 5.4–5 percent for April–September 2020. Chief Economic Advisor Krishnamurthy Subramanian agrees with RBI's realistic assessment of inflation trajectory and is optimistic about headline inflation converging back to core inflation at 4.2–4.5 percent by July–August, 2020.

On February 6, 2020, after the usual three-days deliberations RBI's Monetary Policy Committee (MPC), opted for retaining the base rates unchanged. For some time now, the central bank's bank rate has not been having much influence on interest rates in the financial market. Media and the analysts have been camouflaging this trend by phrases like 'market had already factored in the change' or 'it takes some time to percolate the impact to ground level.' In reality, this tool has lost the influence it had on the rate of 'rent' on resources till the beginning of last decade. This is not to underplay the significance of MPC's professional assessment of the influence of developments in the economy on inflation-related issues. Definitely, the periodic assessments should serve as accelerator and brake in policy formulation.

Equally important is the statement setting out various developmental and regulatory policy measures for strengthening regulation and supervision; broadening and deepening of the financial markets; and enhancing customer education, protection and financial inclusion, issued by RBI simultaneously with the Monetary Policy Statement.

The introductory observation in the Monetary Policy Statement issued by RBI on February 6, 2020 reads:

"On the basis of an assessment of the current and evolving macroeconomic situation, the Monetary Policy Committee (MPC) at its meeting today (February 6, 2020) decided to:

- keep the policy repo rate under the liquidity adjustment facility (LAF) unchanged at 5.15 per cent.

    Consequently, the reverse repo rate under the LAF remains unchanged at 4.90 per cent and the marginal standing facility (MSF) rate and the Bank Rate at 5.40 per cent.

- The MPC also decided to continue with the accommodative stance as long as it is necessary to revive growth, while ensuring that inflation remains within the target.

    These decisions are in consonance with the objective of achieving the medium-term target for consumer price index (CPI) inflation of 4 per cent within a band of +/− 2 per cent, while supporting growth."

    In his address at St Stephen's College, New Delhi on January 24, 2020, RBI Governor Shaktikanta Das dwelt in great detail the evolution of monetary policy in India (See Appendix XVI for excerpts covering the period 2016 onwards).

Concluding the Speech, He Said:

"Monetary policy frameworks in India has thus evolved in line with the developments in theory and country practices, the changing nature of the economy and developments in financial markets. Within the broad objectives, however, the relative emphasis on inflation, growth and financial stability has varied across monetary policy regimes. Although global experience with financial stability as an added policy objective is still unsettled, the Reserve Bank has always been giving due importance to financial stability since the enactment of the Preamble to the RBI Act. The regulation and supervision of banks and non-bank financial intermediaries has rested with the Reserve Bank and has kept pace with the prescribed global norms over time. More recently, the focus of financial stability has not only confined to regulation and supervision but also extending the reach of formal financial system to the unbanked and unserved population.

Apart from financial inclusion, there is also a focus on promoting secured, seamless and real-time payments and settlements. This renewed focus on financial inclusion and secured payments and settlements are not only aimed at promoting the confidence of general public in the domestic financial system but also improving the credibility of monetary policy for price stability, inclusive growth and financial stability.

Joint Effort by RBI and GOI to Manage Liquidity

While committing that efforts are on from government's side to the covenants of the Fiscal & Budget management Act (FRBM) by containing fiscal deficit to agreed levels, responding to a debate in Parliament, Finance Minister Nirmala Sitharaman said that Centre is giving equal importance to all the four growth engines, namely, public investment, private investment, consumption and export. In support, she listed measures such as lowering corporate tax, removing dividend distribution tax, reducing Goods & Services Tax (GST) on electric vehicles, amending the Insolvency & Bankruptcy Code (IBC) for faster disposal of cases and amalgamation of 10 public sector banks into four. Let us be optimistic about government's will to mainstream and deploy nation's domestic assets including equity investments in PSUs for promoting economic growth. One also expects productive use of all reserves including foreign exchange reserves to fetch reasonable return on investments, without depleting their real value.

RBI on its part, has become more active in deploying all weapons of monetary policy management in its armour more judiciously and on an ongoing basis. To support lending to auto, housing and MSME sectors, RBI has given exemption from the requirement to maintain 4 percent

CRR (Cash Reserve Ratio) on deposits equivalent to the incremental loans disbursed by banks to these sectors. The exemption will be effective from the fortnight ended January 31, 2020. The first special lending window with this facility will be open till July 31, 2020. Under the Liquidity management Framework, RBI will also be using instruments like fixed and variable rate repo/reverse repo auctions, outright OMOs, forex swaps and other instruments from time to time.

Appendix XVI (Ref: RBI's Monetary Policy II)

Excerpts from the address by RBI Governor Shaktikanta Das at St Stephen's College, New Delhi on January 24, 2020 (Source: RBI Website)

2016 onwards: Flexible Inflation Targeting

Amid this, a Monetary Policy Framework Agreement (MPFA) was signed between the Government of India and the Reserve Bank on February 20, 2015. Subsequently, flexible inflation targeting (FIT) was formally adopted with the amendment of the RBI Act in May 2016. The role of the Reserve Bank in the area of monetary policy has been restated in the amended Act as follows: "the primary objective of monetary policy is to maintain price stability while keeping in mind the objective of growth."

Empowered by this mandate, the RBI adopted a flexible inflation targeting (FIT) framework under which primacy is accorded to the objective of price stability, defined numerically by a target of 4 per cent for consumer price headline inflation with a tolerance band of +/– 2 per cent around it, while simultaneously focusing on growth when inflation is under control. The relative emphasis on inflation and growth depends on the macroeconomic scenario, inflation and growth outlook, and signals emerging from incoming data. Since then RBI has been conducting monetary policy in a forward-looking manner and effectively communicating its decisions to maintain inflation around its target and thereby to support growth. At the same time, RBI is also fine-tuning its operating procedures of monetary policy for effective policy transmission across the financial markets and thereby onto the real economy. As an outcome, inflation has fallen successively and has averaged below 4 per cent since 2017–18, notwithstanding recent up-tick in inflation driven by food prices, especially the sharp increase in vegetable prices reflecting the adverse impact of unseasonal rains and cyclone.

Evolution of monetary policy in line with the changing Theoretical Developments and International Best Practices

The monetary policy framework in India has also been guided by developments in theory and international best practices. For instance, the collapse of the Bretton-Woods system of fixed exchange rates and high inflation in many advanced economies during the 1970s provided the necessary background to the choice of money supply as a nominal anchor. Since the late 1980s, however, experience of many advanced countries with monetary targeting framework was not satisfactory inter alia due to growing disconnect between monetary aggregates and goal variables such as inflation. A similar instability in money demand function was also evidenced in the Indian context in the 1990s which led to a shift from monetary targeting to multiple indicators approach in 1998.

Since early 1990s, beginning with New Zealand in 1990, many advanced and emerging market economies (EMEs) have switched to inflation targeting as the preferred policy framework. India, however, formally adopted the framework in 2016 which has helped us in terms of learning from the experiences of a diverse set of countries over a long period of time. In fact, the post-global financial crisis experience questioned the relevance of narrow focus on price stability as the sole

objective of monetary policy, which called for adoption of a flexible approach to inflation targeting to achieve macro-financial stability. In this milieu, financial stability has emerged as another key consideration for monetary policy, though jury is still out as to whether it should be added as an explicit objective. It is interesting to note that the central banking function as the lender of last resort (LOLR) has remained intact, notwithstanding the developments and refinements in the policy frameworks across countries, including India.

Evolution of monetary policy in line with the financial market developments

Financial markets play a critical role in effective transmission of monetary policy impulses to the rest of the economy. Monetary policy transmission involves two stages. In the first stage, monetary policy changes are transmitted through the money market to other markets, i.e., the bond market and the bank loan market. The second stage involves the propagation of monetary policy impulses from the financial market to the real economy – by influencing spending decisions of individuals and firms. Within the financial system, money market is central to monetary operations conducted by the central bank.

In the case of India, money market prior to the 1980s was characterised by paucity of instruments and lack of depth. Owing to limited participation, money market liquidity was highly skewed, characterised by a few dominant lenders and a large number of chronic borrowers. In the presence of ad hoc Treasury Bills with fixed interest rate under the system of automatic monetisation, Treasury Bills could not emerge as a short-term money market instrument. Administered interest rates and captive investor base in government securities market further impeded open market operations as an ineffective instrument of monetary control. The prevalence of interest rate regulations along with restrictions on participation prohibited the integration of different market segments which is a prerequisite for effective monetary policy transmission. In this environment, monetary policy initially relied mainly on credit planning and selective credit controls and eventually on monetary targeting through quantitative instruments

Financial markets reforms since the early 1990s, therefore, focused on dismantling various price and non-price controls in the financial system to facilitate integration of financial markets. Reform measures encompassed removing structural bottlenecks, introducing new players/instruments, ensuring free pricing of financial assets, relaxing quantitative restrictions, strengthening institutions, improving trading, clearing and settlement practices, encouraging good market practices and promoting greater transparency. These reforms gradually facilitated the price discovery in financial markets and interest rate emerged as a signalling mechanism. This paved way for introduction of the Liquidity Adjustment Facility (LAF) in 2000–01 as a tool for both liquidity management and also a signalling device for interest rates in the overnight money market. Amid greater integration of domestic financial markets with global markets, subsequently, the RBI also began to recognise the impact of global developments on domestic monetary policy. The developments in financial markets enabled the Reserve

Bank to use market-based instruments of monetary policy and utilise the forward-looking information provided by financial markets in the conduct of monetary policy under the multiple indicators approach.

Although various segments of financial markets had acquired depth and maturity over time, a key challenge has been on fuller and faster transmission of policy rate changes not only to money market segments but also to the broader credit markets. In order to address these challenges, the Reserve Bank has been trying different models. At the same time, the liquidity management framework was also fine-tuned since April 2016 with the objective of maintaining the operating target close to the policy rate. Under this framework, the Reserve Bank assured the market to meet its durable liquidity requirements while fine-tuning its operations to make short-term liquidity conditions consistent with the stated policy stance. This was achieved through a variety of instruments including fixed and variable rate repo/reverse repo of various maturities, the marginal standing facility (MSF) and outright open market operations – complemented at times by the cash management bills and foreign exchange swaps.

Challenges in the Current Context

One of the major challenges for central banks is the assessment of the current economic situation. As we all know, the precise estimation of key parameters such as potential output and output gaps on a real time basis is a challenging task, although they are crucial for the conduct of monetary policy. In recent times, shifting trend growth in several economies, global spillover effects and disconnect between the financial cycles and business cycles in the face of supply shocks broadly explain why monetary policy around the world is in a state of flux. Nonetheless, a view has to be taken on the true nature of the slack in demand and supply-side shocks to inflation for timely use of counter cyclical policies.

We, in the Reserve Bank, therefore, constantly update our assessment of the economy based on incoming data and survey based forward looking information juxtaposed with model-based estimates for policy formulation. This approach helped the Reserve Bank to use the policy space opened up by the expected moderation in inflation and act early, recognizing the imminent slowdown before it was confirmed by data subsequently. Monetary policy, however, has its own limits. Structural reforms and fiscal measures may have to be continued and further activated to provide a durable push to demand and boost growth. In my previous talks elsewhere, I have highlighted certain potential growth drivers which, through backward and forward linkages, could give significant push to growth. Some of these areas include prioritising food processing industries, tourism, e-commerce, start-ups and efforts to become a part of the global value chain. The Government is also focusing on infrastructure spending which will augment growth potential of the economy. States should also play an important role by enhancing capital expenditure which has high multiplier effect.

SECTION III – PROFESSIONALIZING FINANCIAL SYSTEM

PSBs in recovery room: Multiple prescriptions

What do PSBs want?

Prompt Corrective Action (PCA): Need of the hour

Public Sector Banks: Readying to meet new challenges

FDI in Indian Banks

Changing phases of debt restructuring

Handling bank frauds

Strengthen Reserve Bank of India

PSBs in Recovery Room: Multiple Prescriptions

"Repeated government allusions to a $5 trillion economy by 2024, which would necessitate steady real growth of at least 8–9 percent per year starting from now, seem increasingly unrealistic."

-Dr. Raghuram Rajan, former RBI Governor in India Today, December 16, 2019

The quote above is brought here to take on record the timing and selective nature of release of information by economists to pad up the stories they would build up later on. Dr. Rajan, perhaps for the first time, has also spoken at different forums about the legacy inherited by the Prime Minister Narendra Modi's government in 2014 from UPA II. He had this to say, in his article published in India Today:

"A large number of infrastructure projects had stalled because of difficulties in land acquisition, lack of inputs like coal or gas, or the slow pace of obtaining government clearances. Existing power producers were running into difficulties as heavily indebted power distribution companies delayed payments or stopped buying. India experienced the absurdity of surplus power capacity even as power demand went unmet. As more promoters ran into financial distress, bad loans on bank balance sheets increased, slowing the flow of new credit.

The agricultural sector was also in a mess. In part, this resulted from decades of misguided government intervention such as distorted pricing and subsidies—which resulted in anomalies such as a water-short nation exporting water-thirsty rice. In part, this resulted from neglect; successive governments did little to eliminate the hordes of middlemen who took their cut as food travelled from the farm to the fork; instead, governments spent scarce resources on loan waivers, a form of misdirected cash transfer, rather than on improving farmer access to new technologies, seeds or land. Prime Minister Modi was elected, not just because his record in Gujarat suggested he would resolve these legacy issues, but also because he promised reforms that would enhance growth and employment."

Just as fiscal policy measures impact central bank's monetary policy, the legacy issues flagged by Dr. Rajan had a lot to do with the chaotic situation in which the Indian Financial Sector in general, and the Public Sector Banks (PSBs) in particular landed in recent times. We must thank the former RBI governor for taking interest in the progress of reform measures he initiated during his stay in India and sharing his views which have the backing of his experience gained in India and abroad on policy formulation and implementation.

As RBI governor Dr. Raghuram Rajan had mentioned the following as principal reasons for rising NPAs while deposing before the Public Accounts Committee:

- Domestic and global slowdown.

- Delays in statutory and other approvals' especially for projects under implementation.

- Aggressive lending practices during upturn, as evidenced from high corporate leverage.

- Laxity in credit risk appraisal and loan monitoring in banks.

- Lack of appraisal of skills for projects that need specialized skills, resulting in acceptance of inflated cost and aggressive projections.

- Wilful default, loan fraud and corruption.

Have we Forgotten Traditional Principles of Banking?

Kautilya in Arthashastra incorporated risk and uncertainty to the levels of profit and interest. He had indicated that the higher level of risk and uncertainty must be rewarded by higher profits and interests. He prescribed the allowable profits on imports to be twice of that on domestic goods. Allowable profits on imports was 10 percent whereas it was 5 percent on domestic products. The reason behind this was clear. In those days, the importers of foreign goods had to face great danger of being robbed and looted at the time of shipment of the products from other states. Kautilya's concept of profit is quite similar to the modern days profit theory which states that profit is the reward of uncertainty. Kautilya favored charging interests on loans but the rate of interest was regulated by the state. According to him, rate of interest should be determined by two factors – risk involved and productivity of the capital. The rate of interest was higher for the traders however, it was lower for the personal purpose, such as, marriage or funeral etc. purposes. Furthermore, interest rate was different for different types of trades depending on the riskiness of the venture. Hence it is observed that determination of interest rate considered both elements – risk and productivity of the loan. Human consideration of interest payment was also observed. Certain groups of people, such as, inability to pay, students etc. were exempted from paying interest. However, they had to come through proper legal system to avail such exemption. Hence, differentiated interest rate structure depending on the purpose of loan were prevailed at that time which is very much similar to modern days borrowing and lending system of banks and financial institutions (Source: Kautilya's Arthashastra, Sarkar, 2000).

Though the numbers may undergo change, the principles of banking and economics enunciated by Kautilya in Arthashastra hold good even today. We need to revisit the rationale and evolution of banking in India, perhaps over centuries and in more detail the relevance of money lenders during the last century to set right the house of banking in order.

Till deregulation of interest rates, there was some method in madness, in the factoring-in of the principles of cross-subsidization in prescription of interest rates. Post-deregulation, while interest rates on deposits went by the principle of 'demand and supply,' there was inadequate application of mind in deciding interest rates on loans. Those who borrowed heavily, in thousands of crores, influenced, to an extent interest rates policy also and some banks failed to charge higher interests or prescribe conditionalities making mid-term reviews a professional tool to monitor end-use of loans.

Social control and the nationalization of bigger banks that followed gave an impression that banks are another armof government to implement welfare measures. Professionalism took a back seat.

Institutions in the Financial Sector

We need to have a relook at the institutional system in the financial sector in India. We have, during the last one year discussed in some detail the problems faced by commercial banks including public sector banks. At this stage, let us initiate some discussion about cooperative banks and "Non-Banks" which are also facing stressful situation.

Cooperative Banks

The approach to regulating the banking business of cooperatives has been half-hearted ever since 1966 when certain provisions of the Banking Regulation Act 1949 were made applicable to cooperative societies by incorporation of Section 56 in the B R Act.

More than five decades have passed without any serious effort to diagnose and treat the inherent inadequacies in the administrative and supervisory/regulatory architecture that sustains the cooperatives in India. The laxity on the part of legislators in regulating cooperatives professionally is attributable to the vested interests of political parties and local landlords in managing the multiple activities of village level to high profile national level cooperatives.

Since the beginning of last century when cooperative movement emerged on the Indian scene, cooperatives have been playing a proactive role in the economic development and social life in this country. Attempts by vested interests to capture and manage cooperative institutions and resultant efforts to circumvent regulatory and supervisory requirements did affect the growth of this ideal institutional system, off and on, since certain provisions of the Banking Regulation Act, 1949 were made applicable to cooperative societies. The problems faced by cooperative banks during demonetization (2016), the present state of affairs at the Mumbai-based multi-state PMC Bank and the genesis of the ambitious proposal to set up Kerala Bank can be traced to inadequacies in managing cooperatives.

The present initiatives to overhaul cooperatives should, inter alia, keep in view the following:

- Need to separate banking business from other activities undertaken by cooperatives and ear-marking administrative, regulatory and supervisory responsibilities to appropriate agencies. This is necessary as both central and state governments are involved in the administration of cooperatives.

- To retain the cooperative character with members' participation, examine whether Multi-state urban cooperative banks should be made federations of state level units.

- Consider whether it would be advantageous to convert urban cooperative banks, like the proposed Kerala Bank which want to expand business and go commercial and do universal banking as banking companies.

The present challenges add to GOI's and RBI's responsibility to ensure that the dual control (state government having a major role in management matters and RBI's regulatory and supervisory role) does not adversely affect the cooperative institutions' smooth functioning.

"Non-Banks"

For most of the ills in the financial sector, of late, it has become fashionable to blame the Reserve Bank of India(RBI). The role of "Non-Banks" affecting the smooth functioning of the financial system is much more today than, say, a decade before. The IL&FS and DHFL debt default imbroglio and even the failure of Punjab an Maharashtra Cooperative (PMC) Bank can be traced to exploitation of banking system through back-door by "Non-Banks." This issue is being addressed by RBI by prescribing a liquisityrisk management framework for NBFCs and core investment companies (CICs). Simultaneously, RBI has relaxed end-use stipulation under external commercial borrowing framework for corporates and NBFCs.

RBI's Role

Everyone knows inflation-fighting is not and should not be the principal business of Reserve Bank of India. But certain developments during the decade that is coming to an end gave such an impression in the public mind. This feeling was reaffirmed by the legalization of Monetary Policy Committee (MPC) with a given mandate of keeping inflation at 4 plus or minus 2 percent. One cannot blame RBI for its December 2019 MPC decision not to touch base rates, as the inflation was moving nearer to the upper limit of 6 percent. RBI was also aware that, after cutting the policy repo rate by a cumulative 135 basis points in the previous five bi-monthly policy reviews beginning February 2019, the rate transmission down the layers was not to the level expected and it was prudent to pause and watch.

As discussed last month RBI has woken up to the task of infusing order into the institutional system in the financial sector. The statement on Developmental and Regulatory Policies issued along with the Monetary Policy Statement in December 2019 gives sufficient indications to this effect (See excerpts in Appendix XVII).

Appendix XVII (Ref: PSBs in the Recovery Room: Multiple Prescriptions)

Excerpts from the Statement on Developmental and Regulatory Policies issued by Reserve Bank of India on December 6,2019 (Source: RBI)

Primary (Urban) Co-operative Banks – Exposure Limits and Priority Sector Lending

With a view to reducing concentration risk in the exposures of primary (urban) co-operative banks (UCBs) and to further strengthen the role of UCBs in promoting financial inclusion, it is proposed to amend certain regulatory guidelines relating to UCBs. The guidelines would primarily relate to exposure norms for single and group/interconnected borrowers, promotion of financial inclusion, priority sector lending, etc. These measures are expected to strengthen the resilience and sustainability of UCBs and protect the interest of depositors. An appropriate timeframe will be provided for compliance with the revised norms. A draft circular proposing the above changes for eliciting stakeholder comments will be issued shortly.

Primary (Urban) Co-operative Banks – Reporting to Central Repository of Information on Large Credits (CRILC)

The Reserve Bank has created a Central Repository of Information on Large Credits (CRILC) of scheduled commercial banks, all India financial institutions and certain non-banking financial companies with multiple objectives, which, among others, include strengthening offsite supervision and early recognition of financial distress. With a view to building a similar database of large credits extended by primary (urban) co-operative banks (UCBs), it has been decided to bring UCBs with assets of ₹500 crores and above under the CRILC reporting framework.

Comprehensive Cyber Security Framework for Primary (Urban) Cooperative Banks (UCBs) – A Graded Approach

The Reserve Bank had prescribed a set of baseline cyber security controls for primary (Urban) cooperative banks (UCBs) in October 2018. On further examination, it has been decided to prescribe a comprehensive cyber security framework for the UCBs, as a graded approach, based on their digital depth and interconnectedness with the payment systems landscape, digital products offered by them and assessment of cyber security risk. The framework would mandate implementation of progressively stronger security measures based on the nature, variety and scale of digital product offerings of banks. Such measures would, among others, include implementation of bank specific email domain; periodic security assessment of public facing websites/applications; strengthening the cybersecurity incident reporting mechanism; strengthening of governance framework; and setting up of Security Operations Center (SOC). This would bolster cyber security preparedness and ensure that the UCBs offering a range of payment services and higher Information Technology penetration are brought at par with commercial banks in addressing cyber security threats. NBFCs – Peer to Peer Lending Platform (NBFC-P2P)

The Reserve Bank had issued directions for Non-Banking Financial Company-Peer to Peer Lending platform (NBFC-P2P) on October 4, 2017. At present, the aggregate limits for both borrowers and lenders across all P2P platforms stand at ₹10 lakh, whereas exposure of a single lender to a single borrower is capped at ₹50,000 across all NBFC-P2P platforms. A review of the functioning of the lending platforms and lending limit was carried out and it has been decided that in order to give the next push to the lending platforms, the aggregate exposure of a lender to all borrowers at any point of time, across all P2P platforms, shall be subject to a cap of ₹50 lakh. Further, it is also proposed to do away with the current requirement of escrow accounts to be operated by bank promoted trustee for transfer of funds having to be necessarily opened with the concerned bank. This will help provide more flexibility in operations. Necessary instructions in this regard will be issued shortly.

Baseline Cyber Security Controls for ATM Switch application service providers of RBI regulated entities

A number of commercial banks, urban cooperative banks and other regulated entities are dependent upon third party application service providers for shared services for ATM Switch applications. Since these service providers also have exposure to the payment system landscape and are, therefore, exposed to the associated cyber threats, it has been decided that certain baseline cyber security controls shall be mandated by the regulated entities in their contractual agreements with these service providers. The guidelines would require implementation of several measures to strengthen the process of deployment and changes in application softwares in the ecosystem; continuous surveillance; implementation of controls on storage, processing and transmission of sensitive data; building capacity for forensic examination; and making the incident response mechanism more robust.

New Pre-Paid Payment Instruments (PPI)

Prepaid Payment Instruments (PPIs) have been playing an important role in promoting digital payments. To further facilitate its usage, it is proposed to introduce a new type of PPI which can be used only for purchase of goods and services up to a limit of ₹10,000. The loading/reloading of such PPI will be only from a bank account and used for making only digital payments such as bill payments, merchant payments, etc. Such PPIs can be issued on the basis of essential minimum details sourced from the customer.

*Detailed guidelines, where necessary will be issued by December 31, 2019.

What Do PSBs Want?

The "Bad Bank" story is resurfacing, in some form or the other, in different contexts. On July 2, 2018, the Hindu Business Line published a full page feature captioned "'Can ARCs ease banks' burden?." Bureaucracy has its own ways of getting things done in its way and this is the latest example of such efforts. The report is indicative of how vested interests keep certain ideas floating till they could be pushed through. To recap:

The idea of 'Bad Bank' was mooted in Economic Survey 2016–17, then called 'Public Assets Rehabilitation Agency' (PARA). All the reasons for not going ahead with institutionalizing bad assets remain valid today except that the idea now gets support from badly managed banks facing the threat of merger which expect to get another lease of life by transferring a portion of stressed assets to the new entity.

In India, fortunately, big public sector banks which have the major portion of NPAs are big enough to professionally manage their own affairs, if functional parity in management and conduct of business is allowed which their counterparts in the private sector enjoy.

The reality that the concept of an independent institutional arrangement for handling stressed assets of the banking system has built-in features that will be harmful for the financial sector in the long run. The possibility of such a depository of impaired assets acting as a disincentive for professionalizing credit appraisal, credit delivery/ monitoring and recovery systems, which process is on track now, seems to have been taken cognizance of, by the Sunil Mehta Panel which has dropped the idea of 'Bad Bank.'

Outsourcing of responsibilities at certain layers of credit appraisal or super-imposing decisions using ownership rights through back door have already contributed to the present NPA situation in PSBs. Shifting the responsibility for recovery from the lender to another agency goes against the principles of best banking practices. Creating a separate 'pocket' for decaying assets can further weaken the supervisory and regulatory bodies in the financial sector for obvious reasons and the idea should be given a decent burial at this stage.

But, as the growing NPA menace continues to challenge the future of Indian Banking System, GOI and RBI together are making all efforts to contain the damage. One gets an impression that this time around, all stakeholders have woken up from the slumber induced by the reassurances from the owner of PSBs (GOI) that depositors' interests are safe in banks. Having said that, utmost care is needed to ensure that the possible scare in the public mind emanating from the analyses of data on banks' stressed assets (NPAs), magnified by the 'flashes' about scams, do not get blown up out of proportion. Such a situation can adversely affect the already impaired health of the Indian financial system.

Here, a couple of observations made by former RBI Governor Dr. Y V Reddy in a recent speech in Kolhapur are relevant. I quote:

"… The Non-Performing Assets in 1996–97 were 17.8 percent of gross advances and 9.2 percent of Net Advances. These ratios are much higher than what is prevailing today at 11.7 percent and 6.9 percent in 2016–17. They were brought down to 9.4 percent and 4.5 percent in 2002–03, still higher than in 2015–16… There were weak banks, and some public sector banks needed a capital injection. These issues were addressed quietly, gradually and systematically. As a result, the NPAs were down to 2.0 percent and 0.9 percent in 2008–09…"

"… Bank deposits continue to be as safe as they have ever been, as far as private sector banks are concerned. They have adequate capital.

The public sector banks do not have adequate capital to take care of the depositors' interest, but since the majority ownership is that of the government, the deposits are safe. These are not limited liability companies, but institutions established under the law. However, the depositors are protected with the tax-payers money. ..."

As the health of PSBs remained neglected and these institutions were exploited for different purposes by different interest groups, the recent efforts by RBI to use modern diagnostic tools and 'surgical treatment' have brought several uncomfortable realities to the fore. These should be seen as positive signs leading to the infusion of professionalism in the conduct of banking business in India.

The introductory to the "Statement on Developmental and Regulatory Policies" released by Reserve Bank of India simultaneously with the Bimonthly Monetary Policy Statement issued on June 6, 2018 (Appendix XVIII) read as under:

"This Statement sets out various developmental and regulatory policy measures for strengthening regulation and supervision; broadening and deepening financial markets; improving currency and debt management; fostering innovation in payment and settlement system; and, facilitating data management."

As the mainstream media did not take much cognizance of this document published by RBI at its website, let us try a brief recap as the content helps understand why RBI is doing what RBI is doing. The statement covered (a) Increase in Liquidity Coverage Ratio (LCR) carve-out from Statutory Liquidity Ratio (SLR), (b) Changes in procedure/modalities in valuation of State Government Securities and spreading of MTM losses (c) Policy change providing for Voluntary Transition of Urban Cooperative Banks into Small Finance Banks, (d) need to encourage formalization of the MSME Sector, (e) Convergence of Priority Sector Lending (PSL) guidelines for housing loans with Affordable Housing definition under Pradhan Mantri Awas Yojana and (f) Decision to permit Core Investment Companies to invest in Infrastructure Investment Trusts (InvITs) as Sponsors under Regulation and Supervision.

Mehta Panel on NPAs

Last month, through a timely and thoughtful intervention in June 2018, GOI appointed a committee under PNB non-executive chairman Sunil Mehta with the SBI chairman and Bank of Baroda managing director PS Jayakumar as members to study and make recommendations for the resolution of the NPA issue. The Mehta Panel report was accepted by GOI during the first week of July 2018. In a media interaction Union Minister Piyush Goyal, announcing the acceptance of the recommendations explained the future course of action as under:

Independent asset management companies (AMCs) and steering committees will be set up for faster resolution of bad loans in the banking system. The proposal is to set up an asset management company/ alternative investment fund (AIF)-led resolution approach to deal with NPA cases of more than Rs. 5 billion. There are about 200 accounts, each of which owes more than Rs. 5 billion to banks. Their total exposure is about Rs. 3.1 trillion. AIF would raise funds from institutional investors. According to the minister, the AMC, to be set up under AIF framework, will become a market maker and thereby ensure healthy competition, fair price and cash recovery.

The committee has also suggested an asset trading platform for both performing and non-performing assets.

The panel has also suggested a plan for dealing with bad loans up to Rs. 500 million. Under the SME Resolution Approach (SRA), loans up to Rs. 500 million would be dealt using a template approach supported by a steering committee. The panel has recommended that the resolution should be non-discretionary and completed in a time bound manner within 90 days.

The Mehta committee has proposed a Bank Led Resolution Approach (BLRA) for loans between Rs. 500 million and Rs. 5 billion. This segment has an exposure of over Rs. 3 trillion. Under the BLRA approach, financial institutions will enter into an inter-creditor agreement to authorize the lead bank to implement a resolution plan in 180 days. The lead bank would then prepare a resolution plan including empanelling turnaround specialists, and other industry experts for operational turnaround of the asset. In case the lead bank is unable to complete the resolution process within 180 days, the asset would go to NCLT.

The gross non-performing assets (NPAs) of PSBs stood at Rs. 7.77 trillion at end-December 2017. Total NPAs of all banks, including private ones, were a whopping Rs. 8.99 trillion.

After releasing the Mehta Panel report on NPAs, Sunil Mehta mentioned in a media interaction that Rs. 800–900bn would be needed to resolve large toxic loans. The immediate media response to the Mehta Panel report on NPAs resolution is comforting.

Last three years have been stressful for banks, government and the banking regulator. Not only because the efforts to cleanse the financial system from various chronic ills resulted in several weaknesses of the system surfacing or the rising demands on budgetary allocations to support ailing banks. The period also brought to light deficiencies and vulnerabilities in managements of institutions across public and private sectors. During this period the institutional system in the Indian Financial Sector has proved its resilience to withstand pressure and has retained public trust.

Banking being solely dependent on monetary resources, emphasis on ensuring capital adequacy, a reasonable growth in deposits base and flow of credit is natural. Sunil Mehta has arrived at a tentative figure of Rs. 800–900bn to resolve large toxic loans. There will be other demands, besides the likelihood of this figure too rising higher.

Extraordinary situations call for extraordinary solutions. Taking a clue from Mehta's observation that "…the returns on stressed assets are quite different from bio-technology, IT and private equity funds," GOI should consider tapping 'idle domestic assets' for long-term investment in banking sector.

Several individuals and organizations may be holding assets in cash, gold and real estate, a part of which, if allowed to be mainstreamed and invested may partly cover the huge funding need at this juncture. Of course, creating national consensus and building public trust will be an uphill task.

Appendix XVIII (Ref: What Do PSBs Want?)

Excerpts from Statement on Developmental and Regulatory Policies*

This Statement sets out various developmental and regulatory policy measures for strengthening regulation and supervision; broadening and deepening financial markets; improving currency and debt management; fostering innovation in payment and settlement system; and, facilitating data management.

I. Regulation and Supervision

1. Increase in Liquidity Coverage Ratio (LCR) carve-out from Statutory Liquidity Ratio (SLR)

   As per the existing roadmap, scheduled commercial banks have to reach the minimum Liquidity Coverage Ratio (LCR) of 100 per cent by January 1, 2019. Presently, the assets allowed as Level 1 High Quality Liquid Assets (HQLAs) for the purpose of computing LCR of banks include, inter alia, Government securities in excess of the minimum SLR requirement and, within the mandatory SLR requirement, Government securities to the extent allowed by the Reserve Bank under Marginal Standing Facility (MSF) [presently 2 per cent of the bank's NDTL] and under Facility to Avail Liquidity for Liquidity Coverage Ratio (FALLCR) [presently 9 per cent of the bank's NDTL]. For the purpose of computing LCR, it has been decided that, in addition to the above-mentioned assets, banks will be permitted to reckon as Level 1 HQLAs Government securities held by them upto another 2 per cent of their NDTL under FALLCR within the mandatory SLR requirement. Hence, the total carve-out from SLR available to banks would be 13 per cent of their NDTL. The other prescriptions in respect of LCR remain unchanged.

2. Valuation of State Government Securities

   As per extant guidelines on prudential norms for classification, valuation and operation of investment portfolio by banks, the state government securities are valued applying the Yield to

Maturity (YTM) method with a uniform mark-up of 25 basis points above the yield of the Central Government securities (G-Secs) of equivalent maturity.

It has now been decided that the securities issued by each state government should be valued based on observed prices. The valuation of traded state government securities shall be at the price at which they have been traded in the market. In case of non-traded state government securities, the valuation shall be based on the state-specific weighted average spread over the yield of the central government securities of equivalent maturity, as observed at primary auctions. The detailed guidelines to this effect will be issued separately by June 20, 2018.

3. Spreading of MTM losses

    In the wake of spurt in the yields of government securities, banks were given an option to spread, over four quarters, the mark-to-market losses recorded on their investment portfolio during the quarters ended December 2017 and March 2018. It was also required that banks build an Investment Fluctuation Reserve (IFR) of 2 percent of their holdings in the AFS and HFT categories to avoid such eventualities. In view of the continuing rise in yield of government securities as also the inadequacy of time to build IFR for many banks, it has been decided to grant banks the option to spread the mark-to-market (MTM) losses on investments held in Available for Sale (AFS) and Held for Trading (HFT) portfolio for the quarter ending June 30, 2018, equally over a period of four quarters, commencing from the quarter ending June 30, 2018. The circular in this regard will be issued within a week.

4. Voluntary Transition of Urban Cooperative Banks into Small Finance Banks

    The High Powered Committee on Urban Cooperative Banks (UCB), chaired by Shri R. Gandhi, the then Deputy Governor of Reserve Bank, had, inter alia, recommended the voluntary conversion of large Multi-State UCBs into Joint Stock Companies and other UCBs which meet certain criteria into Small Finance Banks (SFBs). Taking these recommendations into consideration, it has been decided to allow voluntary transition of UCBs meeting the prescribed criteria into SFBs. The detailed scheme will be announced separately.

5. Encouraging formalization of the MSME Sector

In February 2018, banks and NBFCs were allowed to temporarily classify their exposures to the Goods and Services Tax (GST) registered Micro, Small and Medium Enterprises (MSMEs), having aggregate credit facilities from these lenders up to ₹250 million, as per a 180 day past due criterion, subject to certain conditions. This was done with a view to ease the transition of MSMEs to the formalized sector post their registration under the GST.

Having regard to the input credit linkages and associated issues, it has now been decided to temporarily allow banks and NBFCs to classify their exposure, as per the 180 day past due criterion, to all MSMEs with aggregate credit facilities up to the above limit, including those not registered under GST. Accordingly, eligible MSME accounts, which were standard as on August 31, 2017, shall continue to be classified as standard by banks and NBFCs if the payments due as on September 1, 2017 and falling due thereafter up to December 31, 2018 were/are paid not later than 180 days from their original due date.

In view of the benefits from increasing formalization of the economy for financial stability, the 180 day past due criterion, in respect of dues payable by GST registered MSMEs from January 1, 2019 onwards, shall be aligned to the extant norm of 90 day past due in a phased manner, whereas for entities that do not get registered under GST by December 31, 2018, the asset classification in respect of dues payable from January 1, 2019 onwards shall immediately revert to the 90 day norm.

Detailed guidelines are being issued separately.

6. Convergence of Priority Sector Lending (PSL) guidelines for housing loans with Affordable Housing definition under Pradhan Mantri Awas Yojana

In order to bring greater convergence of the Priority Sector Lending guidelines for housing loans with the Affordable Housing Scheme, and to give a fillip to the low-cost housing for the Economically Weaker Sections and Lower Income Groups, it has been decided to revise the housing loan limits for PSL eligibility from existing ₹28 lakh to ₹35 lakh in metropolitan centres (with population of ten lakh and above), and from existing ₹20 lakh to ₹25 lakh in other centres, provided the overall cost of the dwelling unit in the metropolitan centre and at other centres does not exceed ₹45 lakh and ₹30 lakh, respectively. A circular in this regard shall be issued by June 30, 2018.

7. Emerging Developments in Low Ticket Housing

After a careful analysis of the Housing Loans data, it has been observed that the level of NPAs for the ticket size of up to Rupees two lakh has been high and is rising briskly. Banks need to strengthen their screening and follow up in respect of lending to this segment in particular. The Reserve Bank is closely monitoring this sector and will consider appropriate policy response such as a tightening of the LTV ratios and/or an increase in the risk weights, should the need arise.

*Source: RBI Website

Prompt Corrective Action: Need of the Hour

The Reserve Bank of India notified a "Revised Prompt Corrective Action (PCA) Framework" for all scheduled commercial banks on April 13, 2017. The PCA Framework was in vogue since 2002 and the revised PCA Framework was for a three-year period commencing April 1, 2017, to be reviewed thereafter. Even prior to 2002, when banks showed signs of incipient sickness, like mismatches in Asset-Liability Management, fall in rate of return, inability to meet statutory requirements relating to maintenance of cash reserves and liquid assets and/or erosion in capital, RBI as banking regulator took cognizance and initiated corrective action. The salient features of revised PCA Framework for Banks are given in Appendix XIX.

Thought of going to the basics first, because the recent media reports give the common man an impression that "PCA" was something new introduced recently by RBI against the wishes of GOI and therefore, is one of the contentious issues in the so called GOI-RBI confrontation post-Viral Acharya speech of October 26, 2018.

PCA is just an improvement of the concept of "narrow banking" or restrictions on operations used to bring back individual banks which became 'sick' due to inefficient management or insufficient resources base to support expanding business. In one form or the other, the concept was in use universally since 1960's. In India, where PCA didn't yield desired results, public interest (read depositors' interest) was safeguarded by RBI/GOI, to the extent possible by voluntary/forced closures/mergers. This has happened in the case of several primary (urban) cooperative banks and the Global Trust Bank in the private sector, in not so distant past.

The background in which the ten plus PSBs which are under PCA now (some of them have recovered health and may be back to normal operations soon) should be studied for correcting the GOI's own approach to institutions in which there is substantial government shareholding. While there is nothing wrong in cross-subsidization among PSUs, indiscriminate demands from profit-making PSUs to part with funds without allowing them to grow or augment their reserves do not augur well for the economy.

I am amused by the overenthusiasm in a section of the media to prove that RBI and GOI are traveling on parallel tracks. In a way, perhaps, some accusations and counter arguments on policy issues may help the concerned sides think differently. But that cannot happen by sensationalizing 'anecdotes' from interactions or speeches on a selective way. Fortunately, RBI has a tradition of sorting out issues with GOI at the highest level and the dialogue is never broken when the regulatory and monetary policy interests appear to be in conflict with the short term fiscal policy targets of GOI. Some of the contentious issues between GOI and RBI have been sorted out in the November Board Meeting of RBI, with agreement to continue dialogue on remaining ones. Please see the press release issued by RBI after the central board meeting on November 19, 2018 (Appendix XX).

Raghuvir Srinivasan (The Hindu, November 20, 2018) has summed up the episode excellently well. I quote:

> "The Reserve Bank of India seems to have carried the day, after all, in Monday's marathon 9-hour board meeting.
>
> Going by the brief statement that it put out, of the six deliveries that it had to play, the RBI has shouldered arms to two—PCA relaxation and capital framework which have been referred for expert study; deftly glanced two more—on liquidity for NBFCs and governance of the central bank—to the next board meet, and effectively fended off the last two bouncers on capital norms and MSME borrowings.

> Interestingly, of the two issues on which the RBI has seemingly conceded, the concessions are minimal and appear mainly designed for optics so that the government can have something to take back to Delhi from Mumbai.
>
> The deferment by a year for a part of the additional capital framework is a small give-away in the face of the Centre's demand for relaxation of the capital ratio itself.
>
> Similarly, the MSME credit recast concession is not a big one considering the demand from the Centre was for easier NPA norms for the sector and more credit flow.
>
> Finally, after all the pre-match sledging, the game seems to have gone off smoothly with both sides playing responsibly."

The subject selected for the A. D. Shroff Memorial Lecture in Mumbai delivered by RBI Deputy Governor Viral Acharya on October 26, 2018 was "The Importance of Independent Regulatory Institutions –The Case of the Central Bank." We will revisit this in coming months.

Dr. Acharya spoke in some detail on Prompt Corrective Action while addressing an elite audience at the Indian Institute of Technology, Bombay on 12th October 2018. Excerpts from the speech titled "Prompt Corrective Action: An Essential Element of Financial Stability Framework" can be accessed at RBI's website. Dr. Acharya sought to explain why the Prompt Corrective Action (PCA) framework of the Reserve Bank of India (RBI) was an essential element of its financial stability framework. Acharya said, 'It (the speech) lays out the case for structured early intervention and resolution by regulators for banks that become under-capitalized due to poor asset quality or vulnerable due to loss of profitability.'

In a recent interview with a financial newspaper, former RBI Governor Dr. Bimal Jalan expressed the view that 'there can be no two views that PCA is desirable because so far we have not taken as many steps as required on NPAs and for handling defaults in the banking sector.' Of course, there could be scope for improvement in content and methods of implementation of PCA package which may have to be institution-specific and subject to close monitoring.

Before proceeding further, let us take note of certain ground level realities about policy formulation and administration of regulatory norms. In India, institutions like Election Commission, Comptroller and Auditor General and Reserve Bank of India commanded respect from central and state governments and were trusted by citizens irrespective of their political or religious convictions. Though after some delay in some cases, the Apex Court's (Supreme Court of India) verdicts were treated as 'law of the land' except in exceptional situations where Centre resorted to overcome or circumvent such verdicts through legislative processes. But, of late, there is a disturbing tendency to resist differences in policy perceptions by public statements, where in-house discussions/ consultations can amicably resolve the differences through informed debates. There is a felt need for restraint on the part of government officials, executives, board members and other stakeholders while making public statements on policy issues affecting sensitive sectors of economy or supervisory or regulatory actions by bodies of which they are representatives. This should not be taken as a lament against sharing of personal perceptions while delivering speeches or responding on the background or impacts of decisions for which one is responsible. They are necessary and desirable especially from transparency angle.

Accept "Prompt Corrective Action" as a Necessary Approach

It is comforting to see that there has been perceptible improvement in the financial health of some of the PSBs placed under PCA. The coming out of those banks will save the face of those who have been pleading for 'relaxations' in the PCA norms. Let us not forget that PCA is about ongoing health check up of institutions and, perhaps, could be adapted for implementation in respect of several other organizations in the financial and industrial sectors.

Appendix XIX (Ref: Prompt Corrective Action: Need of the Hour)

The salient features of revised PCA Framework for Banks

A. Capital, asset quality and profitability continue to be the key areas for monitoring in the revised framework.

B. Indicators to be tracked for Capital, asset quality and profitability would be CRAR/Common Equity Tier I ratio[1], Net NPA ratio[2] and Return on Assets[3] respectively.

C. Leverage would be monitored additionally as part of the PCA framework.

D. Breach of any risk threshold (as detailed under) would result in invocation of PCA.

\multicolumn{5}{c}{PCA matrix – Areas, indicators and risk thresholds}
Area	Indicator	Risk Threshold 1	Risk Threshold 2	Risk Threshold 3
Capital (Breach of either CRAR or CET 1 ratio to trigger PCA)	CRAR – Minimum regulatory prescription for capital to risk assets ratio + applicable capital conservation buffer(CCB) current minimum RBI prescription of 10.25% (9% minimum total capital plus 1.25%* of CCB as on March 31, 2017)	upto 250 bps below Indicator <10.25% but >=7.75%	more than 250 bps but not exceeding 400 bps below Indicator <7.75% but >=6.25%	- - In excess of 312.50 bps below Indicator <3.625%
	And/Or Regulatory pre-specified trigger of Common Equity Tier 1 (CET 1min) + applicable capital conservation buffer(CCB) current minimum RBI prescription of 6.75% (5.5% plus 1.25%* of CCB as on March 31, 2017) Breach of either CRAR or CET 1ratio to trigger PCA	upto 162.50 bps below Indicator <6.75% but >= 5.125%	more than 162.50 bps below but not exceeding 312.50 bps below Indicator <5.125% but >=3.625%	

Asset Quality	Net Non-performing advances (NNPA) ratio	>=6.0% but <9.0%	>=9.0% but < 12.0%	>=12.0%
Profitability	Return on assets (ROA)	Negative ROA for two consecutive years	Negative ROA for three consecutive years	Negative ROA for four consecutive years
Leverage	Tier 1 Leverage ratio[4]	<=4.0% but >= 3.5% (leverage is over 25 times the Tier 1 capital)	< 3.5% (leverage is over 28.6 times the Tier 1 capital)	
*CCB would be 1.875% and 2.5% as on March 31, 2018 and March 31, 2019 respectively.				

i. Breach of 'Risk Threshold 3' of CET1 by a bank would identify a bank as a likely candidate for resolution through tools like amalgamation, reconstruction, winding up, etc.

ii. In the case of a default on the part of a bank in meeting the obligations to its depositors, possible resolution processes may be resorted to without reference to the PCA matrix.

E. The PCA framework would apply without exception to all banks operating in India including small banks and foreign banks operating through branches or subsidiaries based on breach of risk thresholds of identified indicators.

F. A bank will be placed under PCA framework based on the audited Annual Financial Results and the Supervisory Assessment made by RBI. However, RBI may impose PCA on any bank during the course of a year (including migration from one threshold to another) in case the circumstances so warrant.

Mandatory and discretionary actions		
Specifications	Mandatory actions	Discretionary actions
Risk Threshold 1	Restriction on dividend distribution/remittance of profits. Promoters/owners/parent in the case of foreign banks to bring in capital	Common menu Special Supervisory Interactions Strategy related Governance related
Risk Threshold 2	In addition to mandatory actions of Threshold 1, Restriction on branch expansion; domestic and/or overseas Higher provisions as part of the coverage regime	Capital related Credit risk related Market risk related HR related Profitability related Operations related
Risk Threshold 3	In addition to mandatory actions of Threshold 1, Restriction on branch expansion; domestic and/or overseas Restriction on management compensation and directors' fees, as applicable	Any other

Common menu for selection of discretionary corrective actions

1. **Special Supervisory interactions**
   - Special Supervisory Monitoring Meetings (SSMMs) at quarterly or other identified frequency
   - Special inspections/targeted scrutiny of the bank
   - Special audit of the bank

2. **Strategy related actions**

   RBI to advise the bank's Board to:
   - Activate the Recovery Plan that has been duly approved by the supervisor
   - Undertake a detailed review of business model in terms of sustainability of the business model, profitability of business lines and activities, medium and long term viability, balance sheet projections, etc.
   - Review short term strategy focusing on addressing immediate concerns
   - Review medium term business plans, identify achievable targets and set concrete milestones for progress and achievement
   - Review all business lines to identify scope for enhancement/contraction
   - Undertake business process reengineering as appropriate
   - Undertake restructuring of operations as appropriate

3. **Governance related actions**
   - RBI to actively engage with the bank's Board on various aspects as considered appropriate
   - RBI to recommend to owners (Government/promoters/parent of foreign bank branch) to bring in new management/Board

- RBI to remove managerial persons under Section 36AA of the BR Act 1949 as applicable
- RBI to supersede the Board under Section 36ACA of the BR Act 1949/recommend supersession of the Board as applicable
- RBI to require bank to invoke claw back and malus clauses and other actions as available in regulatory guidelines, and impose other restrictions or conditions permissible under the BR Act, 1949
- Impose restrictions on directors' or management compensation, as applicable.

4. **Capital related actions**
   - Detailed Board level review of capital planning
   - Submission of plans and proposals for raising additional capital
   - Requiring the bank to bolster reserves through retained profits
   - Restriction on investment in subsidiaries/associates
   - Restriction in expansion of high risk-weighted assets to conserve capital
   - Reduction in exposure to high risk sectors to conserve capital
   - Restrictions on increasing stake in subsidiaries and other group companies

5. **Credit risk related actions**
   - Preparation of time bound plan and commitment for reduction of stock of NPAs
   - Preparation of and commitment to plan for containing generation of fresh NPAs
   - Strengthening of loan review mechanism
   - Restrictions on/reduction in credit expansion for borrowers below certain rating grades
   - Reduction in risk assets

- Restrictions on/reduction in credit expansion to unrated borrowers
- Reduction in unsecured exposures
- Reduction in loan concentrations; in identified sectors, industries or borrowers
- Sale of assets
- Action plan for recovery of assets through identification of areas (geography wise, industry segment wise, borrower wise, etc.) and setting up of dedicated Recovery Task Forces, Adalats, etc.

6. **Market risk related actions**
    - Restrictions on/reduction in borrowings from the inter-bank market
    - Restrictions on accessing/renewing wholesale deposits/costly deposits/certificates of deposits
    - Restrictions on derivative activities, derivatives that permit collateral substitution
    - Restriction on excess maintenance of collateral held that could contractually be called any time by the counterparty

7. **HR related actions**
    - Restriction on staff expansion
    - Review of specialized training needs of existing staff

8. **Profitability related actions**
    - Restrictions on capital expenditure, other than for technological upgradation within Board approved limits

9. **Operations related actions**
    - Restrictions on branch expansion plans; domestic or overseas
    - Reduction in business at overseas branches/subsidiaries/in other entities

- Restrictions on entering into new lines of business
- Reduction in leverage through reduction in non-fund based business
- Reduction in risky assets
- Restrictions on non-credit asset creation
- Restrictions in undertaking businesses as specified.

Any other specific action that RBI may deem fit considering specific circumstances of a bank.

---

[1] CET 1 ratio – the percentage of core equity capital, net of regulatory adjustments, to total risk weighted assets as defined in RBI Basel III guidelines

[2] NNPA ratio – the percentage of net NPAs to net advances

[3] ROA – the percentage of profit after tax to average total assets

[4] Tier 1 Leverage ratio – the percentage of the capital measure to the exposure measure as defined in RBI guidelines on leverage ratio. (Source: RBI)

Appendix XX (Ref: Prompt Corrective Action)

Press Release dated November 19, 2018 issued by RBI

RBI Central Board meets at Mumbai

The Reserve Bank of India's (RBI) Central Board met today in Mumbai and discussed the Basel regulatory capital framework, a restructuring scheme for stressed MSMEs, bank health under Prompt Corrective Action (PCA) framework and the Economic Capital Framework (ECF) of RBI. The Board decided to constitute an expert committee to examine the ECF, the membership and terms of reference of which will be jointly determined by the Government of India and the RBI. The Board also advised that the RBI should consider a scheme for restructuring of stressed standard assets of MSME borrowers with aggregate credit facilities of up to 250 million, subject to such conditions as are necessary for ensuring financial stability. The Board, while deciding to retain the CRAR at 9%, agreed to extend the transition period for implementing the last tranche of 0.625% under the Capital Conservation Buffer (CCB), by one year, i.e., up to March 31, 2020. With regard to banks under PCA, it was decided that the matter will be examined by the Board for Financial Supervision (BFS) of RBI.

Public Sector Banks: Readying to Meet New Challenges

"The 1980s and early 1990s were a period of great stress and turmoil for banks and financial institutions all over the globe, viz. Brazil, Chile, Indonesia, Mexico, several Nordic countries, Venezuela and USA, etc. In USA, more than 1600 commercial and savings banks insured by the Federal Deposit Insurance Corporation (FDIC) were either closed or given FDIC financial assistance during this period. More than 900 Savings and Loan Associations were closed or merged with assistance from Federal Savings and Loan Insurance Corporation (FSLIC) during 1983 to 1990. The cumulative losses incurred by the failed institutions exceeded US $ 100 billion. These losses resulted in the insolvency and closure of FSLIC and its replacement by the Resolution Trust Corporation (RTC) and the Savings Association Insurance Fund (SAIF)..."

Quoted above are the opening sentences from a discussion paper on "Prompt Corrective Action" circulated by the Reserve Bank of India (RBI) circa 2000. So much has been done by the central bank since then, to keep the banking system in India live and healthy. If some public sector banks are today facing strong criticism from the clientele and the public (taxpayers whose money is being 'diverted' to restore banks' health) in equal measure, half the blame should be shared by their owners, GOI, operated by political leadership which abuses the banking system for various reasons.

In his 2010 book "Fault Lines" Dr. Raghuram Rajan wrote as under:

"In dire crises, some systemically important firms may eat through their capital and be close to failure no matter how good the prior supervision or how ample the equity buffers. If some of their activities are essential to overall economic health, we need to figure out how to "resolve" them – to keep the core business running while imposing appropriate costs on investors. One of the key objectives of the resolution mechanism is to impose appropriate losses on debt holders so that debt holders do not merrily acquiesce equity holders' tail risk taking without demanding an additional risk premium, confident they will be bailed out by the government if necessary."

The policy stance taken by RBI during Dr. Rajan's regime (2013–16) on handling stressed assets of banking system in India need to be attributed to the clear understanding of the mechanics of resolution processes, put in black and white by Dr. Rajan three years earlier to his becoming RBI governor.

N. S. Vishwanathan, Deputy Governor, Reserve Bank of India, in his speech at National Institute of Bank Management, Pune on Fourteenth Convocation on April 18, 2018 (see Box for excerpts) made the following observations about banks' approach in general to handling stressed assets:

"The general approach of bankers to stress in large assets has been one of avoiding the *de jure* recognition of non-performance of such accounts. This is why we have a history of a large number of cases of failed restructuring as the schemes were used for avoiding a downgrade rather than resolving the asset. Prolonging the true asset quality recognition suited both the bankers and the borrowers. The former could make their books look cleaner than they actually were; the latter could avoid the defaulter tag even while, in fact defaulting. Governor had referred to this in his March 14, 2018 speech (https://www.rbi.org.in/home.aspx) as the *borrower-banker nexus*, which may not have a pejorative connotation, but implied that the banks indulged in the proverbial act of extending and pretending. It is instructive to mention here that most cases where the SDR scheme was invoked did not result in change of management, implying that the scheme was used only for the asset classification benefit during the standstill period of 18 months. The strike rate in case of S4A was somewhat better, because there were preconditions to the applicability of the scheme and the Overseeing Committee (OC) ensured strict adherence to the framework upfront. However, the total value of such cases in the overall scheme of things was not that significant."

The above two quotes, hopefully, serve the purpose of clearing the misinformation being spread in the media that the present problems faced by PSBs are new developments previously unknown to the regulator. What has really happened is use of new diagnostic tools for assessing the health of the banking system and insisting enforcement of necessary discipline in sanction of credit and recovery of dues by banks have brought to surface several unhealthy practices indulged by banks to support powerful borrowers in looting depositors' money. Both public sector and private sector banks have been indulging in unhealthy lending practices. Private Sector Banks, as they could be more selective in choice of clientele and were able to hire better professionals, are able to camouflage things and bring out glossy pictures while publishing their accounts and balance sheets. The expectation of all banks has been that their losses will be made good periodically by government, using taxpayers' money.

Banks Under Prompt Corrective Action

The Non-Performing Assets (NPAs) of Public Sector Banks (PSBs) have gone up substantially in recent times, forcing RBI to put them under Prompt Corrective Action (PCA). Currently half the total number of PSBs is under PCA framework, which includes Dena Bank, Allahabad Bank, United Bank of India, Corporation Bank, IDBI Bank, UCO Bank, Bank of India, Central Bank of India, Indian Overseas Bank, Oriental Bank of Commerce and Bank of Maharashtra.

Owner Responds

Finance Minister Piyush Goyal in a recent interaction with the senior executives of the 11 public sector banks placed under the Prompt Corrective Action (PCA) framework of the Reserve Bank of India (to check the deteriorating financial health of these banks) told that GOI will extend help to strengthen these banks to come out of PCA framework as quickly as possible. Goyal added that the government will prepare an action agenda on a case-by-case basis, with help of Department of Financial Services, to resolve the issues. The minister said that his meeting with the bankers was very useful to understand what had transpired over the last 12–13 years in the banking system and the heads of the 11 banks shared some very good ideas in the meeting to resolve the crisis.

Eye Opener

The recent cash crunch which resulted in ATMs in several areas in India going dry prompted SBI's Economic Research Department probe into the reasons for shortage of cash when currency in circulation did not go down drastically. The findings of the study include:

- Rs2000 notes were not being circulated enough, especially in states like Bihar and Gujarat and in the southern states;

- ATM withdrawals in the second half of 2017–18 were unusually high;

- Currency velocity (the rate at which currency should be circulating in the market) was on decline resulting in lesser 'cash in hand' with banks;

- The Research Team was not convinced about the reasons like marriage season, harvest etc. for cash crunch as those are not particular to 2017–18.

CFA Statement

Smelling a conspiracy to destroy Public Sector Banks (The Global ANALYST has repeatedly talked about the step-motherly treatment meted out to PSBs, falling short of calling it a conspiracy!), the Centre for Financial Accountability (CFA), an independent platform has submitted to Finance Secretary (GOI) and RBI on April 28, 2018 a public statement accusing the government of hatching a well-orchestrated game plan to destroy public sector banks. According to reports, the statement has been signed by 95 eminent individuals belonging to civil society, bank associations and civil rights associations.

Lack of professionalism in formulation and implementation of some of the recent RBI/GOI initiatives to reform the banking system has invited scathing criticism from the signatories of the above statement. They include demonetization and post-demonetization currency management, Financial Resolution and Deposit Insurance (FRDI) Bill, ATM cash crunch (an aftermath of outsourcing operations of ATMs) and adhocism in levying service charges by banks. Attributing motives and calling it 'a multi-pronged attack on the people, the public sector banks and the economy at large,' the statement asserts that "This cannot be brushed aside as an outcome of mismanagement or wrong policies of government, regulators and bank management. It appears to be a part of a well-orchestrated and deliberate effort to cause mistrust in public sector banks, dismantle their networks and pave the way for privatizing the public banks."

Minus the terse 'trade union' language, the statement conveys a clear message for managers and regulators of public sector banks. 'First Aid' solutions like infusing capital or sending out 'guidelines' will not take them out of the present mess which is not their creation.

FDI in Indian Banks

"Since generations, we have believed that all resources and all wealth belong to the Nature and the Almighty. We all including the Presidents, and Prime Ministers; Kings and Queens are just the trustees or managers of this wealth. The biggest recent advocate of this trusteeship philosophy was Mahatma Gandhi;

Gandhi Ji also used to say there is enough in Nature for your Need; but not for your greed; Due to this belief, we have learnt to live in a way that is conducive to existence of man vis a vis man as well as Nature; which is conducive to the needs of today as well as next generations;

There are teachings, techniques and teachers to guide and guard us so that a false sense of ownership does come in our mind. This only eventually leads to greed, pride and ego (lessons on Gyan and Vairagya);"

-Excerpts from Prime Minister Modi's address at WEF, 2018

Banking is about management of monetized resources. Today, besides ensuring territorial security and internal peace, governance concerns include optimizing deployment of nation's resources for economic development. With globalization came the additional burden of ensuring smooth exchange of resources and skills on a need-based basis between nations. Banks have an integral role in economic development and can play a part in pooling of savings from any part of the world and making them available in any other part, provided the countries create conducive environment for their activities in respective countries. When it comes to mobilization and deployment of resources in a different country, governments generally look at reciprocity mainly concerning legal and regulatory issues in regard to banking business.

Some recent media reports suggest that the Union government is mulling the possibility of increasing foreign investment limits in private sector banks to 100%, from the present 74%, and hiking the foreign investment cap for public sector banks (PSBs), from the present 20% to 49%.

Once the government takes a view, before proceeding further, the finance ministry may consult Reserve Bank of India (RBI). As foreign banks can open wholly owned subsidiaries in India, opening another window for full ownership of existing private sector banks could be suicidal for Indian private sector.

According to the government's current policy, foreign investors—foreign direct investment, foreign institutional investors, and non-resident Indians combined—can invest up to 74% of paid-up capital in private sector banks. While up to 49% foreign investment is allowed under the automatic route, such investments between 49 and 74% require the government's nod under the present norms. The present foreign investment limit of 74% in private sector banks was fixed, with certain sub-limits and conditions of prior GOI approval for investments beyond 49 percent, by GOI in 2004. The sub-limits were removed during the second half of 2015.

The limit covers foreign investment directly in primary market and acquisition through stock market. Regulatory restrictions prevent threats to ownership of banks.

Besides FII, ADR/GDR, Promoters' Contribution and investments by NRIs which are also reckoned for the purpose of monitoring adherence with the ceilings fixed for foreign stakes in the capital of banks.

Banks like HDFC and ICICI had almost touched the ceiling of 74 percent much earlier. The following table gives the position in respect of six private sector banks as of September 2015:

Percentage share of FII and FDI in the share capital of major private sector banks

Bank	FII	ADR/GDR	Promoters' Contribution	Others (NRIetc)	Total
Axis	42.13	3.87	0.00	0.26	46.26
HDFC	32.40	18.87	21.57	0.29	73.13
ICICI	38.24	29.05	0.00	0.29	67.58
IndSind	42.78	10.92	14.98	0.87	69.55
Kotak	34.67	0.01	0.00	12.44	47.12
Yes	41.26	0.00	0.00	0.61	41.87

In the recent past, there were occasions when banks like HDFC had crossed the 74 percent ceiling and RBI had issued notifications preventing further foreign investment in shares of such banks. Such situations had also caused volatility in the equity market not confined to the specified banks. More transparency and perhaps a warning system when the percentage enters a closer figure to the ceiling may help avoid such volatility in the market.

When a proposal to increase foreign investment limit to 100% in private sector banks was mooted in 2015, RBI reportedly raised objections on grounds of "regulatory problems." Now, it seems the issue is being discussed within the finance ministry only, as of now.

When we consider foreign investment in the business of banking in India, a clear distinction should be drawn between foreign ownership in Indian banks and presence of foreign banks doing business in India. In the later case, for regulatory reasons RBI encourages wholly owned subsidiary(WOS) route rather than allowing more branches of foreign banks in India. Rationale for this approach is that the branches of foreign banks are not separate legal entities whereas subsidiaries are locally incorporated separate legal entities. Subsidiaries being locally incorporated have their own capital base and their own local board of directors. In the case of branches, parent banks are, in principle, responsible for their liabilities.

GOI is presently favourably inclined to attracting more foreign direct investment in select sectors. Prime Minister Narendra Modi welcoming such investment made this observation in his address in January 2018 to World Economic Forum in Davos:

"In this direction, we have also undertaken bold FDI reforms. More than 90% of the FDI approvals have been put on the automatic approval route. As a result of these changes, there has been a sharp rise in FDI in the past three years—from 36 billion US Dollars in 2013–14 to 60 billion US Dollars in 2016–17."

Viewed in this context, the objective of the present proposal to raise the limits for FDI in banks seems to be to raise more capital for growth of banking. Naturally, those who will want to come in will prefer banks which do not have any problem in attracting capital like HDFC bank. The move will lead to transfer of full ownership and control to foreigners. In a geo political environment like now, for India this may not be the right thing to do. The grounds which justified nationalization of banks during last century, like the reluctance of banks in private sector to finance social sectors or small borrowers and refusal to open branches in rural and semi-urban areas are still relevant. When the management shifts fully to foreign hands, there can be practical difficulties in enforcing domestic regulations in the conduct of business by banks. Perhaps the regulatory problems against hike in the FDI investments in banks cited by RBI in 2015 are inclusive of these issues.

Balance of convenience lies in continuing with the present norms for foreign direct investment in Indian banks.

Changing Phases of Debt Restructuring

A notification issued on February 12, 2018 to banks by the Reserve Bank of India advising revised framework for Resolution of Stressed Assets justified the change asunder:

"The Reserve Bank of India has issued various instructions aimed at resolution of stressed assets in the economy, including introduction of certain specific schemes at different points of time. In view of the enactment of the Insolvency and Bankruptcy Code, 2016 (IBC), it has been decided to substitute the existing guidelines with a harmonized and simplified generic framework for resolution of stressed assets."

In effect, RBI has replaced several loan restructuring schemes with a strict 180-day timeline by when banks need to finalize a resolution plan in case of default, failing which the account will be referred for bank.

RBI has mentioned that the extant instructions on resolution of stressed assets such as Framework for Revitalising Distressed Assets, Corporate Debt Restructuring Scheme, Flexible Structuring of Existing Long Term Project Loans, Strategic Debt Restructuring Scheme (SDR), Change in Ownership outside SDR, and Scheme for Sustainable Structuring of Stressed Assets (S4A) stand withdrawn with immediate effect and accordingly, the Joint Lenders' Forum (JLF) as an institutional mechanism for resolution of stressed accounts also stands discontinued. It is clarified that the accounts, including such accounts where any of the schemes have been invoked but not yet implemented, shall be governed by the revised framework.

The purpose obviously is 'harmonizing existing guidelines with the norms specified in the Insolvency and Bankruptcy Code (IBC), 2016.

The new guidelines have specified a framework for early identification and reporting of banks' stressed assets. The revised guidelines have the following salient features:

a. As part of the revised framework, banks will be required to identify initial stress in loan accounts, immediately on default, by classifying stressed assets as special mention accounts (SMA) depending upon the period of default.

b. All lenders will be required to put in place Board-approved policies for resolution of stressed assets, including timelines for resolution.

c. As soon as there is a default in the borrower entity's account with any lender, all lenders – singly or jointly – shall initiate steps to cure the default.

d. All accounts, including those where any of the schemes have been invoked but not yet implemented, will be governed by the revised framework.

Restructuring is an act in which a lender, for economic or legal reasons relating to the borrower's financial difficulty grants concessions to the borrower. Restructuring would normally involve modification of terms of the advances/securities, which may include, among others, alteration of repayment period/repayable amount/the amount of installments/rate of interest; roll over of credit facilities; sanction of additional credit facility; enhancement of existing credit limits; and, compromise settlements where time for payment of settlement amount exceeds three months.

The guidelines recognize that the resolution plan (RP) may involve many actions/plans/reorganization including, but not limited to, regularization of the account by payment of all overdues by the borrower entity, sale of the exposures to other entities/investors, change in ownership, or restructuring.

All lenders have been advised by RBI to put in place Board-approved policies for resolution of stressed assets under this framework, including the timelines for resolution. As soon as there is a default in the borrower entity's account with any lender, all lenders – singly or jointly – shall initiate steps to cure the default.

The revised guidelines also specify the timelines for resolution of stressed assets asunder:

"If a resolution plan in respect of large accounts is not implemented as per the timelines specified, lenders will be required to file insolvency applications, singly or jointly, under the IBC within 15 days from the expiry of the specified timeline."

All lenders will be required to submit a Central Repository of Information on Large Credits (CRILC) on all borrower entities in default with aggregate exposure of Rs. 5 crore and above. The CRILC-Main Report is to be submitted on a monthly basis effective April 1, 2018. In addition, the lenders shall report to CRILC all borrower entities in default, on a weekly basis, at the close of business on every Friday, or the preceding working day if Friday happens to be a holiday.

Reserve Bank of India has decided to do away with the Joint Lenders' Forum (JLF) as an institutional mechanism for resolution of stressed accounts.

Timelines for Large Accounts to be Referred under IBC

In respect of accounts with aggregate exposure of the lenders at 2000 crore and above, on or after March 1, 2018, including accounts where resolution may have been initiated under any of the existing schemes as well as accounts classified as restructured standard assets which are currently in respective specified periods as per the previous guidelines, RBI has prescribed timelines for implementing RP asunder:

i. If in default as on the reference date, then 180 days from the reference date.

ii. If in default after the reference date, then 180 days from the date of first such default.

The RBI guidelines *inter alia* state that any failure on the part of lenders in meeting the prescribed timelines or any actions by lenders with an intent to conceal the actual status of accounts or evergreen the stressed accounts, will be subjected to stringent supervisory/enforcement actions as deemed appropriate by the Reserve Bank, including, but not limited to, higher provisioning on such accounts and monetary penalties.

The timing of issue of the more strict guidelines on the subject by RBI is being debated in the media. The now famous comment by Dr. Raghuram Rajan on demonetization which referred to 'short-term losses off-setting the long-term gains' is being rephrased and used in the context of the new guidelines on NPAs. Those who find fault with the timing say that the revised framework may 'prove disastrous' as the country is just recovering from the twin policy blows of demonetization and GST implementation. Though such arguments go well with the purpose of postponing pain, one need to also concede that the three policy initiatives on Note-Ban, GST and NPAs are to solve three different problems which are independent, though the impact will be on the same people.

Here, I am forced to abruptly break this article, as the 'breaking news' about RBI's quick action to get clarity on regulatory preventive measures to handle daylight robberies in banks using credit-route as has happened in what is now known as PNB SCAM has to be covered this month itself.

Malegam-led Panel on NPA Divergence and Bank Frauds

In what is being lauded as a swift response from the regulator to the shocking revelations after the surfacing of grave irregularities in compliance with prudential norms in credit-related operations in PNB resulting in a multi-crore scandal affecting the credibility of the banking system, RBI has, on February 20, 2018, decided to constitute an Expert Committee under the chairmanship of Shri Y H Malegam, a former member of the Central Board of Directors of RBI, to look into the reasons for high divergence observed in asset classification and provisioning by banks vis-à-vis the RBI's supervisory assessment, and the steps needed to prevent it; factors leading to an increasing incidence of frauds in banks and the measures (including IT interventions) needed to curb and prevent it; and the role and effectiveness of various types of audits conducted in banks in mitigating the incidence of such divergence and frauds.

The members of the committee will be: Shri Bharat Doshi, Member, Central Board of Directors, RBI; Shri S Raman, former Chairman and Managing Director, Canara Bank and former Whole-Time Member, SEBI; and Shri Nandkumar Saravade, Chief Executive Officer, Reserve Bank Information Technology Pvt Ltd (ReBIT). Shri A K Misra, Executive Director, RBI will be the Member-Secretary of the committee.

In a press release issued announcing the appointment of the Malegam Panel, RBI mentioned that, as part of its ongoing efforts for strengthening of the supervisory framework in the country, Bank has been issuing necessary instructions to banks from time to time on a variety of issues of prudential supervisory concern, including the management of operational risks inherent in the functioning of banks. According to RBI, "The risks arising from the potential malicious use of the SWIFT infrastructure, created by banks for their genuine business needs, has always been a component of their operational risk profile. RBI had, therefore, confidentially cautioned and alerted banks of such possible misuse, at least on three occasions since August 2016, advising them to implement the safeguards detailed in the RBI's communications, for pre-empting such occurrences. Banks have, however, been at varying levels in implementation of such measures."

In the wake of SWIFT-related fraud involving significant amount, reported recently by Punjab National Bank, RBI reiterated its confidential instructions and mandated the banks to implement, within the stipulated deadlines, the prescribed measures for strengthening the SWIFT operating environment in banks. Explaining the context for appointment of Malegam Panel, RBI noted the large divergences observed in asset classification and provisioning in the credit portfolio of banks as well as the rising incidence of frauds in the Indian banking system.

Handling Bank Frauds

"It is not entirely surprising that there has been a recurring theme in report after report on financial sector reforms in the country that has suggested strengthening of PSB governance through improvement in top management and Board member appointments; or, ownership neutrality in banking regulatory powers; or improving market discipline by considering a variety of diverse ownership structures."

RBI Governor on March 14, 2018

The quote below is from the letter dated April 29, 2009 addressed to Union Minister for Corporate Affairs by Shri Vepa Kamesam, Chairman, Expert Committee to advise Government on issues concerning the Serious Fraud Investigation Office (SFIO) after finalizing the Expert Committee Report:

"Corporate Fraud is a highly complex phenomenon and is one of the many consequences of rapidly growing economy characterized by increasing number of corporate entities with a wide range of activities and each across several markets. Any case of serious fraud has devastating consequence on confidence of investors, credibility of the corporate sector, financial survival of company and its employees, losses to banks and financial institutions and setback to economy as a whole. As elsewhere in the world, the Indian corporate world has also been afflicted by various frauds starting with stock market scams of 1990's and early 200's to accounting fraud in the case of Satyam. While the earlier frauds had an impact on Indian stock market, the latest accounting fraud perpetrated by promoters of Satyam was a fraud on the company itself as it endangered the very survival of the company. The impact of serious and complex frauds on a large number of stakeholders has intensified the concern for effective regulation of the corporate world."

This can apply mutatis mutandis today to banks and financial sector in the context of PNB SCAM. I leave the rephrasing and rewriting of Kamesam's observations by appropriate substitution of words like corporate entities and corporate sector by banks and financial sector to the readers, or perhaps the Malegam Panel (appointed by RBI) which is already on the job of looking into NPA divergence and bank frauds.

SFIO had interaction with chiefs of ICICI Bank, Axis Bank and PNB during the third week of March 2018 as part of their probe into the PNB SCAM.

RBI is continuing preventive action and follow up of earlier initiatives to tighten supervisory and regulatory interventions to ensure smooth functioning of the banking system in the medium term.

As an interim measure, during the third week of March 2018, RBI announced discontinuance of Letters of Undertaking (LoUs) and Letters of Comfort (LoCs) for Trade Credits which were being issued by banks as permitted by RBI in November 2004. This covers the practice of issuance of LoUs/LoCs for Trade Credits for imports into India by AD Category –I banks.

RBI has allowed continuance of issue of Letters of Credit and Bank Guarantees for Trade Credits for imports into India, subject to compliance with the RBI stipulations relating to "Guarantees and Co-acceptances." RBI has also clarified that the revised instructions are without prejudice to permissions/approvals, if any, required under any other law.

Former RBI Deputy Governor Usha Thorat, writing in Mint on March 5, 2018 (PNB fraud: strong action, communication needed), observed:

"It is critical that the RBI and government speak with one voice on both fronts"

Continuing, she said "The Punjab National Bank (PNB) fraud has left everyone shocked. How could a few lower level officers manage to defraud the bank of such large amounts? Had all kinds of internal controls failed? Could it have happened without the knowledge of the higher levels of authority? There are many unanswered questions, although the extent of reporting and discussion in the media is massive."

The article has raised several relevant questions on why the fraud remained undetected for so long and commented on possible lapses. As the media has discussed the subject extensively and for fear of repetition, we will skip further discussion on how's and why's for now and wait for the report of the expert panel looking into the fraud.

Post-PNB SCAM, the lobby which has all along been demanding privatization of public sector banks has intensified its efforts. In an article published in The Hindu Business Line on March 8, 2018, Srinivas Dindi, in a short but thought-provoking piece, covered several aspects which did not justify further privatization of banking business in India at this juncture.

Let us concede that in India, since Nehruvian days, when 'public sector' commanded much more respect than today also, there has been a sponsored lobby out to annihilate public sector undertakings by any means available. We have witnessed the fall of institutions like UTI.

Methods used included creating legal hurdles in parity in functional matters with the private sector, ensuring weaknesses in top management by interference in top-level appointments and HR issues using Government's ownership rights and sometimes by allowing infiltration of people of doubtful integrity at higher levels.

As regards banking in India, as the source of funds and the clientele served by the public sector and private sector banks are the same, there should not have been much difficulty in providing a level playing field for both categories of banks.

But, in reality, only the private sector banks enjoyed functional autonomy to do business on their own terms (choice of clientele, freedom to operate where they want, no interference in HR-related matters including top-level remunerations and so on) within the overall contours of legislative restrictions.

Public sector banks are made answerable to their masters in Finance Ministry, accept responsibility for providing credit for all government-sponsored programs and ensure G Secs are fully subscribed whenever central and state governments entered the market. Of course in making government borrowings successful they have other public sector organizations like LIC which are expected to support the government on an ongoing basis.

By privatization, are we talking about handing over the banks to Mallyas and Modis who are running away with banks' funds? Or are we aiming at professionalization of Indian Banking System, irrespective of ownership? These are choices to make fast. Time is running out.

Owner and Regulator

Recently, "Check for fraud in NPAs above Rs. 500 mn: Govt" was a headline in newspapers. On the face of it there is nothing extraordinary in 'owner' of a business giving operational instructions to the staff working under him. GOI as owner, has the responsibility to ensure smooth functioning of PSBs and the recent developments have shaken the public trust in PSBs, which need to be restored quickly.

But in the given situation, the divergent instructions flowing from GOI and RBI will confuse the already strained managements of PSBs. More likely, they will start waiting for instructions from North Block even after getting operational or supervision-related instructions from RBI, as it is the Finance Ministry which decides the fate of the top management in PSBs.

This is an embarrassing situation for the country's central bank which shoulders the responsibility of working under the RBI Act and administering Banking Regulation as legally mandated under the Banking Regulation Act,1949.

All these and more led to some sharing of mind by RBI Governor Dr. Urjit Patel on March 14, 2018. He said that "Banking Regulatory Powers in India are NOT Ownership Neutral" (See Appendix XXI)

If GOI is not comfortable with the speed with which instructions are percolating down to banks from RBI, they should have a dialogue between them (GOI and RBI) and sort out issues. It is not in public interest for the two being seen talking differently and GOI sharing concerns in the media even before taking the banking regulator into confidence. Owner and Regulator have different kinds of responsibilities. Earlier this is conceded, the better for the image of the Indian Financial System which is already sagging. If banking gets affected by ego-related issues, the fall will be total and there will not be any public sector-private sector divide.

Appendix XXI (Ref: Handling Bank Frauds)

Banking Regulatory Powers in India are NOT Ownership Neutral*

All commercial banks in India are regulated by the RBI under the Banking Regulation (BR) Act of 1949. Additionally, all public sector banks are regulated by the Government of India (GoI) under the Banking Companies (Acquisition and Transfer of Undertakings) Act, 1970; the Bank Nationalization Act, 1980; and the State Bank of India Act, 1955. Section 51 of the amended BR Act explicitly states which portions of the BR Act apply to the PSBs, most common thread across the omissions being complete removal or emaciation of RBI powers on corporate governance at PSBs:

1. RBI cannot remove directors and management at PSBs as Section 36AA (1) of the BR Act is not applicable to the PSBs.

2. Section 36ACA(1) of the BR Act that provides for supersession of a Bank Board is also not applicable in the case of PSBs (and regional rural banks or RRBs) as they are not banking companies registered under the Companies Act.

3. Section 10B(6) of the BR Act that provides for removal of the Chairman and Managing Director (MD) of a banking company is also not applicable in the case of PSBs.

4. RBI cannot force a merger in the case of PSBs as per Section 45 of the BR Act.

5. PSB's banking activity does not require license from RBI under Section 21 of the BR Act; hence, RBI cannot revoke a license under Section 22(4) of the BR Act as it can in the case of private sector banks.

6. RBI cannot trigger liquidation of PSBs as per Section 39 of the BR Act.

7. Furthermore, in a remarkable exception of sorts, in some cases there is duality of Managing Director and the Chairman – they are the same – implying the MD is primarily answerable only to himself or herself.

*Excerpts from RBI Governor Dr. Urjit Patel's speech of March 14, 2018 at Ahmedabad Source: RBI

Strengthen Reserve Bank of India

There appears to be a concerted effort from several quarters to stifle Reserve Bank of India. This is nothing new, and political leadership and bureaucracy had different reasons at different times to pursue a love-hate relationship with India's central bank. Government of India's discomfort with RBI found expression in the Financial Sector Legislative reforms Commission's (FSLRC) report which made recommendations close to suggesting dismantling of RBI's structure and disarming the central bank. FSLRC spent its resources and time in reinventing RBI. Had it devoted half its energies in going into the need for real financial sector reforms relating to structural, administrative and skill and HR-related reforms of the institutional structure in the Financial Sector, the maladies now in the fore including NPA menace would have been handled efficiently during 2013–16 when Dr. Raghuram Rajan was RBI Governor.

The latest reports in the media about a discussion on RBI's dividend policy need to be seen in the above context. In the 80 plus year old history of RBI, there were several situations where mutual support has helped RBI and GOI manage monetary and fiscal policy objectives. RBI Governor's taking Finance Ministry into confidence on policy issues or the details of pre-budget consultations with RBI were not issues of media debates.

As regards RBI's dividend policy, the expectations from the central bank about transfer of RBI's surplus income are made very clear in the Reserve Bank of India Act, 1934. Section 47 of the Reserve Bank of India Act, 1934 dealing with RBI's surplus income reads as under:

"47. Allocation of surplus profits. After making provision for bad and doubtful debts, depreciation in assets, contributions to staff and superannuation funds 2[and for all other matters for which provision is to be made by or under this Act or which] are usually provided for by bankers, the balance of the profits shall be paid to the Central Government."

While RBI may ultimately succumb to pressure and accommodate GOI's wishes, strength of the central bank is also about its strong balance sheet and any measure to dilute RBI's reserves position (as a percentage to balance sheet total RBI's reserves have come down from a near 12 in 2009 to below 8 last year) will weaken the central bank further. Needless to say, that will reduce RBI's ability to support GOI in times of need. Writing on the subject in The Hindu Business Line long back, RBI's former Deputy Governor S S Tarapore had observed:

"The building up of the contingency reserves is particularly is important as the Government is in no position to pick up the losses once the contingency reserve is wiped out. One of the saddest events that can occur is the death of a central bank. This has happened in some countries and the RBI can never be too careful."

Contents of the Malegam Committee (2013) will not throw sufficient light on the circumstances under which RBI skipped transfer of funds to contingency reserves during the three years when Dr. Raghuram Rajan was RBI Governor. The Committee reportedly certified adequacy of reserves for 'three years' and also recommended building up of contingency reserves!

There is another document which gives arguments that support the need for a strong RBI Balance Sheet. On the last day of his three year tenure as Governor in RBI (September 3, 2016), Dr. Raghuram Rajan spoke on "The Independence of the Central Bank" addressing the students of the St Stephen's College, New Delhi. He included the speech in his 2017 book "I Do What I Do" with the following brief introductory:

"As I entered my last few days in office, I wanted to leave explaining why an independent central bank was necessary in India. An invitation from St Stephen's College, which has produced so many good economists in India, was the ideal venue. There was one specific issue I wanted to clarify, the RBI dividend. Despite paying the largest amount the RBI had ever paid to the government as dividend during my term as Governor, there was still constant suggestions that we could pay more. Some of these suggestions reflected an inadequate understanding of the economics at work in a central bank's balance sheet. On my last day in office, 3 September 2016, I addressed both issues."

Please see excerpts from the above speech quoted in the Appendix XXII.

The concerns expressed and the guidance given by Dr. Raghuram Rajan in the above speech could be the starting point for any discussion on RBI's dividend policy.

Appendix XXII (Ref: Strengthen Reserve Bank of India)

First Year Economics: There is no free lunch. RBI Dividend Policy

A fundamental lesson in economics is there is no free lunch. This can be seen in the matter of the RBI dividend: Some commentators seem to suggest that public sector banks could be recapitalized entirely if only the RBI paid a larger dividend to the Government. Let me explain why matters are not so simple.

If what follows is complicated, trust me, it is. But pay attention, students, especially because it is about your money. I am sure you will understand. How does the RBI generate surplus profits?

We, of course, print the currency held by the public, as well as issue deposits (i.e. reserves) to commercial banks. Those are our fixed liabilities. As we issue these liabilities, we buy financial assets from the market. We do not pay interest on our liabilities. However the financial assets we hold, typically domestic and foreign government bonds, do pay interest. So we generate a large net interest income simply because we pay nothing on virtually all our liabilities.

Our total costs, largely for currency printing and banker commissions, amount to only about $1/7^{th}$ of our total net interest income. So we earn a large surplus profit because of the RBI's role as the manager of the country's currency. This belongs entirely to the country's citizens.

Therefore, after setting aside what is needed to be retained as equity capital to maintain the creditworthiness of the RBI, the RBI Board pays out the remaining surplus to the RBI's owner, the Government.

The RBI Board has decided it wants the RBI to have an international AAA rating so that RBI can undertake international transactions easily, even when the Government is in perceived difficulty – in the midst of the Taper Tantrum, no bank questioned our ability to deliver on the FCNR(B) swaps, even though the liability could have been tens of thousands of crores. Based on sophisticated risk analysis by the RBI's staff, the Board has decided in the last three years that the RBI's equity position, currently around 10 lakh crores, is enough for the purpose. It therefore has paid out the entire surplus generated to the Government, amounting to about Rs. 66,000 crores each in the last two years, without holding anything back. This is of the order of magnitude of the dividends paid by the entire public sector to the Government.

In my three years at the RBI, we have paid almost as much dividend to the government as in the entire previous decade. Yet some suggest we should pay more, a special dividend over and above the surplus we generate. Even if it were legally possible to pay unrealized surplus (it is not), and even if the Board were convinced a higher dividend would not compromise the creditworthiness of the RBI, there is a more fundamental economic reason why a special dividend would not help the Government with its budgetary constraints.

Here's why: Much of the surplus we make comes from the interest we get on government assets or from the capital gains we make off other market participants. When we pay this to the government as dividends, We are putting back into the system the money we made from it – there is no additional money printing or reserve creation involved. But when we pay a special dividend to the government, we have to create additional permanent reserves, or more colloquially, print money.

Every year, we have in mind a growth rate of permanent reserves consistent with the economy's cash needs and our inflation goals. Given that budgeted growth rate, to accommodate the special dividend we will have to withdraw an equivalent amount of money from the public by selling government bonds in our portfolio (or alternatively, doing fewer open market purchases than we budgeted). Of course, the Government can use the special dividend to spend, reducing its public borrowing by that amount. But the RBI will have to sell bonds of exactly that amount to the public in order to stick to its target for money creation.

The overall net sale of Government bonds by the Government and the RBI combined to the public (that is, the effective public sector borrowing requirement) will not change. But the entire objective of financing Government spending with a special RBI dividend is to reduce overall Government bond sales to the public. That objective is not achieved!

The bottom line is that the RBI should transfer to the government the entire surplus, retaining just enough buffers that are consistent with good central bank risk management practice. Indeed, this year the Board paid out an extra 8,000 crores than was promised to the Government around budget time.

Separately, the government can infuse capital into the banks. The two decisions need not be linked. There are no creative ways of extracting more money from the RBI– there is no free lunch! Instead, the Government should acknowledge its substantial equity position in the RBI and subtract it from its outstanding debt when it announces its net debt position. That would satisfy all concerned without monetary damage.

If what I have said just now seems complicated, it is, but it is also the correct economic reasoning. Similar detailed rationales lead us to turn down demands to cut interest rates in the face of high inflation, to depreciate or appreciate the exchange rate depending on the whim of the moment, to use foreign exchange reserves to fund projects, to display forbearance in classifying bad loans or waived farmer loans as NPAs, and so on…

We have been tasked with a job of maintaining macroeconomic stability, and often that task requires us to refuse seemingly obvious and attractive proposals. The reason why we have to do what we have to do may not be easy for every unspecialized person, even ones with substantial economics training, to grasp quickly.

Of course, we still must explain to the best of our ability but we also need to create a structure where the public trusts the central bank to do the right thing. This then is why we need a trusted independent central bank.

**This is not strictly true. Our earnings on foreign exchange assets come from outside the system, so when we pay this to the Government as dividend, we are printing additional money. We do account for this.

*Excerpts from remarks by Raghuram G Rajan, Governor, Reserve Bank of India on September 3, 2016 at St Stephen's College, New Delhi.

Source: RBI Website

www.ingramcontent.com/pod-product-compliance
Lightning Source LLC
Chambersburg PA
CBHW030926180526
45163CB00002B/474